"As a veter   e pet lover, I
believe i   ies to heal.
This bo   wise information, compassionate reflection, and practical h⋯ for honoring and memorializing the life of your pet."

— Dr. Marty Becker, resident veterinarian on
ABC's *Good Morning America* and author of
Chicken Soup for the Pet Lover's Soul

"Let me say this about *Saying Goodbye to Your Angel Animals*: I love it. I treasure it. The Andersons have left no question unposed, no conflict bypassed, no reflection unacknowledged. If you are facing or have faced the loss of a beloved animal friend, let this book be your companion and your comfort. There exists no better exploration of this landscape of loss."

— Susan Chernak McElroy, author of
Animals as Teachers and Healers and *Why Buffalo Dance*

"In this latest offering, the Andersons prove themselves to be the very angels and divine messengers of hope they write about in their Angel Animals series. Helping readers to understand and successfully navigate the turbulent waters of grief, they remind us that the bond of love between a human soul and an animal soul is never broken and that the spiritual connection that binds us with a beloved animal never dies. *Saying Goodbye to Your Angel Animals* is fine reading for those who seek to better understand the agony of pet loss and a priceless gift of compassion and love for anyone anticipating or coping with the loss of a cherished animal companion."

— Marty Tousley, certified hospice bereavement counselor
specializing in pet loss and author of
Children and Pet Loss and The Final Farewell

"Allen and Linda Anderson care about those who have experienced loss. With warmth and sincerity, they provide many suggestions and resources to help you through the healing process. *Saying Goodbye to Your Angel Animals* inspires and brings comfort to anyone who has lost a beloved animal companion."

— Niki Behrikis Shanahan, author of
The Rainbow Bridge: Pet Loss Is Heaven's Gain
and There Is Eternal Life for Animals

Saying Goodbye to Your Angel Animals

ALSO BY ALLEN AND LINDA ANDERSON

Angel Animals: Divine Messengers of Miracles

Angel Cats: Divine Messengers of Comfort

Angel Dogs: Divine Messengers of Love

Angel Dogs with a Mission: Divine Messengers in Service to All Life

Angel Horses: Divine Messengers of Hope

God's Messengers: What Animals Teach Us about the Divine

Rainbows and Bridges: An Animal Companion Memorial Kit

Rescued: Saving Animals from Disaster

Saying Goodbye to Your Angel Animals

Finding Comfort After Losing Your Pet

Allen & Linda Anderson

New World Library
Novato, California

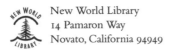 New World Library
14 Pamaron Way
Novato, California 94949

Text design by Tona Pearce Myers

Library of Congress Cataloging-in-Publication Data
Anderson, Allen.
Saying goodbye to your angel animals : finding comfort after losing your pet / Allen and Linda Anderson.
     p.   cm.
"Originally published in 2005 as part of a boxed set titled Rainbows & Bridges"—T.p. verso.
Includes bibliographical references.
ISBN 978-1-57731-626-8 (pbk. : alk. paper)
1. Pet owners—Psychology. 2. Pets—Death—Psychological aspects. 3. Bereavement—Psychological aspects. I. Anderson, Linda C.. II. Anderson, Allen.- Rainbows & bridges. III. Title.
SF411.47.A53 2008
155.9'37—dc22   2008015743

First printing as *Saying Goodbye to Your Angel Animals*, August 2008
ISBN 978-1-57731-626-8
Printed in the United States on 50% postconsumer-waste recycled paper

g New World Library is a proud member of the Green Press Initiative.

10 9 8 7 6 5 4 3 2 1

To Mugsy, Prana, Feisty, Sparkle, Taylor, and Vanessa's Babette

Contents

Friends at the Rainbow Bridge

Oh! Friend, who gave and comforted, who knew
So overwell the want of heart and mind,
Where may I turn for solace now, or find
Relief from this unceasing loss of you?

— Theodosia Garrison, "The Closed Door"

Bottom line: It hurts like crazy. And hardly anybody under-stands. Family, friends, co-workers sympathized. For a while. But they expected that you would be over it by now. Maybe they found a day or even a week of grieving to be acceptable. But after all, this was only a pet. Why are you still moping around? Why don't you get another one? Why don't you get a life?

So you ingest their words or their silent disapproval like vials of poison to your self-esteem. You wonder if they could be right. Are you a hopeless, codependent, overly romantic, anthropomor-phizing weakling? Why do you mourn the loss of your animal companion more than any other loss in your life? How can this bereavement cause such emptiness, grayness, and sheer torture? You feel foolish. You are embarrassed. You don't want to admit the magnitude, intensity, or tenacity of your pain. You are tempted to suck it in, shove it under, seal it over.

You yearn for a gentle paw to touch your cheek, a sweet chirping to greet each day, an exercise buddy to pad along beside you, or penetrating eyes with childlike innocence to watch your every movement — just one more time.

Despite the lack of understanding from others, you realize that the life and death of your animal companion must not — will not — be forgotten. The brilliant light that illuminated the darkest corners of your life has to be honored. You have lost a way of living as well as a dear friend. And it may be one of the most debilitating losses you have ever experienced.

Besides, you are a person who gives credit where credit is due. You long to acknowledge that an animal companion brought love, joy, comfort, tolerance, respect, balance, companionship, and meaning to your life in ways that are unique, admirable, and worthy of remembering.

Now, you are ready to read this book.

YOUR PARTNERS IN GRIEVING

We are Allen and Linda Anderson, authors of books about the spiritual connection between people and animals. We are a married couple who have been blessed with two human children and many furry family members. Over the twenty-five years of our marriage, we have gone through the losses of Prana, Feisty, Mugsy, Taylor, and Sparkle. We have buried them, scattered their ashes, held memorial services, missed them, and mourned them. We have grieved with our children and each other. We have wondered if the hole that was left when our animal companions died would ever be filled. We have walked through the valley of the shadow of death into the sunlight once again.

In our work with the Angel Animals Network, which we founded in 1996 to increase love and respect for all life through the power of story, we have received thousands of stories from readers who have struggled to find their way out of the maze of sadness that confused them after a pet died. From their experiences and our own, we have fashioned a kind of framework for your grieving and healing. Grief is messy, so we are describing for you the process of organic grieving. It allows you to relax into the knowledge that grief isn't organized. It has its own natural cycles and timetable. As you read through the chapters, empathize with the stories of others, and do the exercises and meditations, your grieving will take on new meaning. You will have the opportunity to transform into a more spiritually self-aware person and, in time, feel happiness again. Our hope is that you will emerge from bereavement as one who looks at life through the clear, bright eyes of love.

YOU HAVE HISTORY

We once did a radio interview during which a caller telephoned the station with a story about a parrot who had recently been left at an animal shelter. The parrot sat at the front desk with staff members and volunteers, who were busily processing adoptions. Throughout the shelter, the bird's voice was heard wailing plaintively, "What went wrong? What went wrong?"

This bird asked an age-old question. Throughout history, human beings have turned to ritual, prayer, and commemoration to deal with their grief when a pet died and to figure out what went wrong. Ancient people's memorial practices helped them to mourn. Egyptians mummified their pets with the same chemicals and in the same ways as they did humans. The grieving family members shaved their eyebrows when a pet died and buried the animal in the family crypt. Persians, as well as people of other ancient cultures, established pet cemeteries for their companion animals. Native Americans shared their dwellings with and welcomed animals into their tribes. They called upon animal spirits during their vision quests.

Like golden threads, animals have always been woven into the tapestry of humans' lives. For many, especially children, the loss of a pet is a first and profound experience with death's mysterious presence. An animal's passing evokes questions about the significance of the animal-human relationship, the afterlife, the soul, and God. Your longing to find answers, explanations, and consolation may bring you to a spiritual turning point. An animal's death can cause you to feel doubt, disbelief, and disconnection. Whirlwinds of anger and denial may compound your grief and cut you off from normal avenues of community and religious solace. When others don't understand that grief for your devoted animal friend is as real and painful as any other kind of grief, you may find yourself feeling even more isolated and alone.

YOU HAVE FRIENDS WHO UNDERSTAND

This book is designed to serve as a friend who knows how you feel, doesn't judge you, and wants to help you allow grief to follow its natural course into acceptance. We have chosen to express the process of grieving, reconciliation, and healing by using symbolic imagery of the legendary Rainbow Bridge. Some truly magnanimous and wise person wrote a story that has since comforted millions of us after our animal companions have died. No one knows who the author is. Yet we all feel grateful for the story's messages of hope.

THE RAINBOW BRIDGE

Just this side of heaven is a place called the Rainbow Bridge.

When an animal dies who has been especially close to someone here, that pet goes to the Rainbow Bridge. There are meadows and hills for all of our special friends, so they can run and play together. There is plenty of food and water and sunshine, and our friends are warm and comfortable. All the animals who had been ill and old are restored to health and vigor; those who were hurt or maimed are made whole and strong again, just as we remember them in our dreams of days and times gone by.

The animals are happy and contented, except for one small thing: they miss someone very special to them who had to be left behind.

They all run and play together, but the day comes when one suddenly stops and looks into the distance. The bright eyes are intent; the eager body quivers. Suddenly he begins to break away from the group, flying over the green grass, his legs carrying him faster and faster. *You* have been spotted, and when you and your special friend finally meet, you cling together in joyous reunion, never to be parted again. The happy kisses rain upon your face;

your hands again caress the beloved head, and you look once more into the trusting eyes of your pet, so long gone from your life but never absent from your heart.

Then you cross the Rainbow Bridge together...

RAINBOWS AND BRIDGES

The first three chapters of this book will help you to recognize the primary colors of the Rainbow Bridge. These colors of blue, red, and yellow represent sadness, remembrance, and spiritual growth. Observing and nourishing yourself with the rainbow's colors will allow you to become peaceful. You will begin to understand how the loss of your animal companion has affected your life physically, emotionally, psychologically, and spiritually.

The next four chapters offer bridges that will transport you through the mourning process. These bridges symbolize a metaphoric range from the practical to the mystical. They are bridges that commemorate and honor the life and death of your pet. Like the Rainbow Bridge, they take you and your animal companion to a place where you can be reunited spiritually. Throughout this book, you will read about the experiences of people who have seen the rainbow's colors and crossed the bridges before you. Their stories offer knowledge, comfort, and wisdom.

One such story is Joanne Nobrega's. When her children were little, Joanne found what she calls the "dog of my heart." Her family adopted a fluffy, energetic, nipping, and challenging five-month-old yellow Lab named Brandy. This dog saw Joanne's children through their growing-up years. When Joanne's sons left home, Brandy remained to fill her and her husband's empty nest.

After fifteen years of Brandy's love and friendship, the dog developed kidney disease. One sad Thanksgiving Day, Joanne and her husband stayed home to cuddle on the floor with their dying pet, stroking his velvet ears, and praying for the strength to say goodbye to him. On the following Saturday, the family lit a candle, formed a circle around Brandy, and loved him as the dog passed away.

Brandy's death unbalanced Joanne like nothing she had ever experienced. She began to wonder if the weight of her grief was normal. At last she had to, as she put it, "lean into the pain instead of fighting it any longer."

Joanne's sadness that year was deepened by an exceptionally wet, gray winter. She looked out her window at the places where Brandy used to play and prayed to see a rainbow. Thinking of the Rainbow Bridge story, she believed that such a rainbow would be the sign she needed to reassure her that Brandy was now part of the essence of life.

For days after her initial prayer, Joanne continued to stand at her bay window and search the skies in hope of finding a rainbow. An absence of the answer to her prayer only added to her pain.

Joanne writes:

One especially dreary afternoon I picked up a set of pictures that had just been developed, but these were not just any pictures. They were the last ones we had taken with our dear pet on the day before he died. I came home, sat at the kitchen table, and dropped the package in front of me. I wanted to see them, but at the same time, I trembled at the thought of viewing Brandy's tired, worn face, alive then and gone now.

I peeled open the package. One by one, I drank in the sweet brown eyes staring back at me. Memories of him flooded my thoughts. I noticed that there were other pictures of Brandy I had not remembered taking. As I looked at them through my tears, I heard my own gasp break the silence of my empty house. Right there, across Brandy's head and his velvet ear, was a rainbow. He had been lying under a skylight. The reflection of the glass painted my answered prayer across his brow.

This was the moment; this was my encounter with my Comforter. The glow of the rainbow warmed my heart with the promise that had been given. I knew that I was not, and never would be, left alone. I had my sign that all was well, that in the whole scheme of life, this was not out of God's plan. This was the cycle of life, birth, death, and renewal.

Seeing a rainbow in the sky would not have had the same impact as the rainbow's colors pressed like a halo over my precious dog's head. I will always remember that day at my kitchen table. The day the promise was given, the day my yellow Lab became my "Rainbow Dog."

HOW THIS BOOK IS DESIGNED

The material in this book runs the gamut; it will be just as useful to those who have a humanist or secular philosophy of life as it will be to those who actively practice a religion or spiritual path. You have the right and the responsibility to decide what and how much you want to take from these pages. Listen to your heart and your inner guidance. Use only what makes you comfortable and helps you to feel better. Discard or disregard the rest.

We have created three types of memorial service that you can use as written, add to, delete from, or mix and match. If the words in these services say what you want to say, by all means read them. If they don't reflect your thoughts, feelings, and beliefs, change them in any way that suits you and the guests you invite to your ceremony.

Meditations and questions at the end of each chapter offer prompts for further reflection to help you sort out your thoughts, feelings, and experiences as you go through the grieving process. Additional meditations and exercises are scattered throughout this book so you can immediately reflect and expand upon key points. In the Appendix there are even more meditations that give specific thoughts and suggested activities for more completely healing your grief. We encourage you to use the prompts and meditations for writing about the loss of your animal friend and to start a journal or scrapbook where you can preserve special photographs and mementos.

We use the terms *animal companion* and *pet* interchangeably, because in our vocabulary, *pet* is a term of endearment. We do not use the terms *owner* or *master*, because we respect animals as partners and companions of humans in this world. We don't believe that you can own animals. Their love and devotion are freely given, and no price you pay to have them in your life could ever be enough.

We alternate between referring to animals as male or female rather than using only the referent *he*. And we don't refer to animals with *it* or *that*, as if animals were objects instead of sentient beings.

Because you are an individual and your circumstances and views of life are unique, no one can fully comprehend exactly what you are experiencing with the loss of your pet. It is our sincerest hope, though, that as you read these pages, you will find yourself in the company of compassionate listeners and understanding friends.

You, your animal companions, the people who have contributed their thoughts and stories, and we are poised now to journey to the Rainbow Bridge together. Peace and acceptance are on the other side. Happiness and joy in celebrating a life well lived await you.

Hold our hands. We offer them to you in friendship. We will cry with you. We will remember with you. We will honor and commemorate with you.

Let love always be your guide. For unlike the physical bodies we miss so dearly, love never dies.

MEDITATION

How My Life Would Have Been Different

By thinking about how different my life would have been without you, I feel even more gratitude for the gifts you have given me.

There were times when I would have chosen another course of action or changed directions had it not been for the wise and gentle counsel of your example.

- What role did you play as a divine messenger for me?
- When did you influence my decisions with your gentle ways?
- How did you help me to be a kinder person?

MEDITATION

The Rainbow Bridge Reunion

The Rainbow Bridge stretches across the expanse between life and death. In the Rainbow Bridge story, the bridge is said to link heaven and earth.

My dear friend, you are waiting for me at the Rainbow Bridge. Someday, after we have greeted each other, we will walk together to the other side. There we will celebrate and honor our forever friendship.

How do I imagine our reunion?

What will I feel when we meet at the Rainbow Bridge?

Rainbows
The Colors of Saying Goodbye

What skillful limner e'er would choose
To paint the rainbow's varying hues,
Unless to mortal it were given
To dip his brush in dyes of heaven?

— Sir Walter Scott, "Marmion"

CHAPTER ONE

Rainbow Blue
Organic Grieving

I miss the little wagging tail;
I miss the plaintive, pleading wail;
I miss the wistful, loving glance;
I miss the circling welcome-dance.

— Henry Willett, "In Memoriam"

A light has left your world — the light of innocence, of friend-ship, of a love that did not restrict or bind. Consequently, the loss of your animal friend may mean that the intensity of sadness you feel is greater than any you have ever known. This is why it is so important to allow yourself to grieve and heal in your own way and time.

ORGANIC GRIEVING

You are an individual. The animal who shared your life was an in-dividual. Death or loss of an animal is a one-time experience.

Grieving is an ongoing passage toward healing and reconciliation. In *Kindred Spirits*, Dr. Allen Schoen writes, "Grief has no timetable. It is a journey filled with peaks and valleys. Just when you think you are getting over your loss, a fresh wave of pain pulls you back. But grieving is part of the human experience; it is a journey to a new stage of life."[1]

Because you are unique, we suggest that you engage in what we call *organic grieving*. With organic grieving there is only one rule or guideline for mourning: *use whatever naturally alleviates your stress and pain without harming yourself or anyone else or breaking any laws.*

Organic grieving enables you to find the most effective and natural ways to restore yourself and rebuild your life after the loss of a beloved animal companion. This means giving yourself permission to mourn loss in ways that originate from your essence, your spirit, your unique self. Organic grieving emanates from the core of your being, where the essence of what you honestly feel and believe about life and death resides. There are no "shoulds" or "have-tos" with organic grieving. You simply do not allow anyone to take away your right to grieve in ways that fit most naturally with your physical, emotional, psychological, and spiritual makeup.

Your methods and the amount of time it takes for you to grieve and to heal may look strange to someone who isn't inside your skin or who hasn't loved as you have loved. So be it. You don't have to justify your thoughts and feelings over the loss of a pet. We wholeheartedly agree with what the pet bereavement counselor and author Jamie Quackenbush says in *When Your Pet Dies*. He writes, "Experience your emotions, don't fight them or judge them, and ignore people who try to do that for you. No matter who you are, your bereavement over a pet's death is necessary, a natural process that will help you in the long run."[2]

RAINBOW BLUE

Blue represents the color of your sadness and grief. Rainbows linger after storms, their colors brightening a once gloomy sky. Short waves of white light create the inner edge of a rainbow by penetrating raindrops and reemerging as the color blue. Yet to see the rainbow's brilliant colors, we must be standing with our backs to the sun.

Like the rainbow's shortest waves, animal companions are white lights who are with us only for a comparatively brief amount of time. While on earth, they have reflected back our best and wisest selves. Now a beloved pet's death has blotted out the sun and revealed the blue of sadness with alarming clarity. Blue becomes the first color of the rainbow that we see. Organic grieving will help you experience the blue of sorrow in a natural way.

PHASES OF ORGANIC GRIEVING

Many excellent books and research studies have shown that human beings tend to experience a set of emotions and follow a pattern of behaviors that can be grouped into what are known as the stages of grief. It's good to know about these stages and their characteristics, so if you go into a rage around your house and kick wastebaskets against the wall after your pet dies, you'll know that you aren't going crazy. Anger is one of the stages of grief — a normal reaction to loss.

By not imposing any preconceived ideas about what you should be feeling at a given time after a loss, organic grieving gives you leeway to experience whatever you want at the point when it naturally occurs. The thoughts and feelings of a particular phase can last for a minute or a month. Various aspects of grief may pop up like jack-in-the-boxes when you least expect them. For example, it's normal to feel shock, numbness, and denial as an initial reaction to the death of a loved one. It's also normal not to feel any of those things until much later, or to experience them repeatedly in varying waves of intensity.

Organic grieving follows your natural rhythms for handling pain and loss. When you're upset, do you usually cry? Lash out at others? Do you grow quiet and withdrawn? Is your first reaction to turn to God or pray for strength? Grieving organically will enable you to let your natural impulses run their course rather than trying to box yourself into an "acceptable" stage of grief for a "reasonable" period of time. An understanding of organic grieving will also help you to deal with possible incongruent grieving among your family members — that is, the possibility that you won't all grieve in exactly the same way. Although you and your spouse, for example, may both be hurting mightily over the loss of your family pet, you could be grieving organically in entirely different ways. That can make you feel out of sync with or judgmental about each other, even though both of you have been deeply affected by the loss.

In the next few sections, we list some of the most prevalent stages of grieving that experts on the subject have agreed are common, with a few examples of how each stage might manifest itself after the loss of an animal companion. But again, remember, however you normally react to loss is your own organic way of grieving.

Shock, Doubt, and Denial

This is the "I can't believe my friend is gone" phase of grieving. It's nature's way of boarding over the windows to keep the high winds of grief and loss from shattering the glass and blowing through the house. But those boards of denial also keep you temporarily from seeing the reality of the storm. Shock, doubt, and denial can take the form of prolonging the suffering of an animal when you can't allow yourself to believe that it's time to let go. After the loss, this aspect of grieving can leave you walking around in a daze, unable to accept that your pet is gone. Customary habits, such as picking up the dog's leash before going for a walk or expecting to wake up to a raspy pink tongue licking your arm, are still as real to you as they were when your animal companion was alive.

Denial, shock, disbelief, even skepticism are natural reactions to pet loss. These feelings can be worsened if you didn't get to see the animal after death or if the pet has wandered off or been stolen. You may not have had enough closure to convince yourself that the animal won't be returning. When reality is too harsh and painful, it's a natural survival mechanism to refuse to admit that your worst fears have come true.

But when does denial become dysfunctional?

The pet bereavement counselor and author Julia A. Harris writes in *Pet Loss: A Spiritual Guide*, "Denial becomes abnormal when an individual is convinced that some action can be performed to bring back the lost life. I do not refer here to the belief in a life after death. Considering your pet spiritually alive and ascending toward divinity for reincarnation, transmutation, or resurrection, and believing that communication with your pet is possible, [do] not indicate denial of the fact that your pet has crossed the threshold from physical existence into the realm of death."[3] A more hard-nosed therapist or veterinarian might not give you so much leeway on the subject of the normal range of denial, but we tend to agree with Julia Harris. If you know your pet's physical body is dead, but you have felt a continuing spiritual presence, that doesn't mean you're in denial. You may be experiencing, firsthand, the knowledge that even death cannot extinguish the love and the spirit of an animal.

Anger, Confusion, Resentment, and Blame

Anger takes many forms. You could be mentally making a list of everyone, including yourself, whom you hold responsible for your animal companion's death. Your thinking could be muddled and confused as you try to make sense out of something that, right now, seems senseless. Resentment may be consuming you with its ability to keep at bay the more debilitating emotion of heart-wrenching sadness. You might be unreasonably irritated with friends, co-workers, or strangers. You could feel irrational anger toward the pets in your family who lived while another died and, consequently, withdraw from the surviving animals.

In chapter 5, we'll talk more about anger and how to deal with it. For now, suffice it to say that it's important to recognize, accept, and release anger in constructive ways. Activities such as punching pillows, writing in a journal about your rage, and screaming where no one can hear you allow angry and resentful feelings to dissipate naturally.

Guilt, Bargaining, and Regret

It's almost impossible for someone who has loved and lost a pet not to feel guilty and have regrets. Upon the death of the animal, you might find yourself wondering if you did everything you could have. Did I feed the animal the right food? Did I provide the best and safest environment? Did I let the animal suffer too long or too much? The questions go on and on. Yet dwelling upon your regrets causes despair and guilt to deepen.

To ward off regret, blame, and guilt, you may have tried to bargain with the vet, with the animal, or with God in an effort to prolong your pet's life. Perhaps you cried and pleaded for your best friend not to leave. In anticipatory grief, you may have attempted to stave off the terrible sadness and loneliness that you knew were coming. The professional bereavement counselor Wallace Sife, PhD, writes in *The Loss of a Pet*, "By having to become the angel of death to that beloved pet and extension of ourselves, we are each tasting a bit of our own death, which is always upsetting. We are realistically forced back into the aloneness of our life journey, despite all the friends and family we may have."[4]

Guilt and regret can overwhelm you years after the loss of your pet. Sandra, a subscriber to our online newsletter, *Angel Animals Story of the Week*, wrote about what she considered to be one of the most difficult decisions she ever had to make. Her dear animal companion of fifteen years, a dog named Bear, had struggled to combat a hyperthyroid condition for almost two years. By then,

Bear had lost a quarter of her hair. The dog was constantly hungry and miserable, losing weight, and wailing with pain most of the time. After doing everything she could to keep Bear alive and depleting her financial resources in the process, Sandra had to struggle with whether to have the dog euthanized.

Even though Sandra believed that Bear would be in a better place after death, she worried and felt guilty about euthanasia. Years later, she continued to wonder whether she had done the right thing. She wrote, "I looked up the word euthanasia and learned that it comes from Greek for *easy death*. God, I hope so. I did not want Bear to suffer anymore." Sandra closed her letter by asking our readers to let her know what they thought about the practice of euthanasia. We received an avalanche of responses. The following readers' answers may help if you are dealing with guilt or regret over choosing to euthanize your pet.[5]

Diana from Australia wrote, "Congratulations. What courage, compassion, and love you have. It reflects in your words and deeds. If I were an animal in your care, I would be so content with my life. Bear would have loved you all the more for giving her the life and love you did."[6]

A letter from Rita comforted Sandra by explaining how she had talked to her pug, Betty, after the dog could no longer stand up or move. Rita wrote, "I told Betty I had to put her to sleep and that she can come back to me."[7]

Dee expressed what many of our readers believe about euthanasia. She wrote, "I know it was the right thing to do. Sometimes, it's the last, best, most loving gift we can give our animal friends, to free them from their painful, failing bodies and let their spirits soar. I also believe that they will be with us in eternity. They're waiting for us in heaven or at the Rainbow Bridge. Though it may, and does, break our hearts, we can rest in the knowledge that we were unselfish at the end and did what was best for them."[8]

Most of our readers were in agreement that euthanasia was necessary to end an animal's pain and opted for quality of life over longevity. Some even wished that euthanasia would be an option for humans. However, a Buddhist practitioner named Trisha wrote to express a differing opinion. Trisha said, "From the Buddhist standpoint, we may do our companion animals a disservice by creating karma for them by prematurely taking their lives."[9]

On the other hand, sometimes people are too quick to choose euthanasia as a solution to their problems with a pet. We receive calls and letters from people who want us to help them ease their conscience over the decision to euthanize a perfectly healthy pet. Known as *convenience euthanasia*, this practice is painful for everyone, including the veterinarian who must decide if he or she should do it. Most often, the desire to end a healthy animal's life comes about because of behavioral problems, such as the pet urinating in the wrong place at the wrong time or not being obedient enough. We try to help people find alternatives to euthanasia under these circumstances. With the wide range of assistance available through animal therapists, animal communicators, and veterinary specialists, or the possibility of someone else adopting the pet, euthanasia is hardly the best choice for an animal who happens to be frustrating a human.

In reading through the books and resources on pet loss, we've noticed that in an attempt to ease their readers' guilt and regret, some authors go overboard with their belief that animals and humans don't have the same attitudes toward death, and animals don't fear dying. Animals try to survive when death is being imposed upon them prematurely. Several accounts of cows and pigs escaping slaughter have made international news. A volunteer who worked at an animal shelter that practices euthanasia on animals if they haven't been adopted by a certain time, told us that she often witnessed dogs straining at the leash and fighting against being taken into the "euthanasia" room.

Usually, though, when an animal has been suffering, he won't cling to life unless the person to whom he is devoted isn't ready to let him go. Then the animal often prolongs his suffering until he senses that the person can release him. The pet psychic Sonya Fitzpatrick writes in *What the Animals Tell Me*, "We must let our animal companions go when their time comes. The greatest gift we can give dying pets is to send them on their way with our love and blessing so that they may make the transition from this earth plane with dignity and peace. If our grief at the thought of their death and our fear of what life will be like without them are so unmanageable that we cannot let our pets go, we cause animals that are in horrible pain to hang on and on, just to please us. That is a terribly irresponsible and unfeeling thing to do."[10]

What to Do with Regrets and Guilt

No matter how you look at it, whether you chose to end your animal companion's suffering or prolong his life, you're likely to regret something. And what if later you realize that you didn't do everything possible to keep your pet alive and healthy? Perhaps you have more information now than you did when you decided to opt for euthanasia. Or perhaps you're looking back at a previous stage of your life and wondering, "What was I thinking?"

A sixty-year-old woman named Barbara wrote to us about a moral dilemma she faced years ago. The decision she made had filled her with regret, and she longed to ease her guilt. Barbara said that after her husband of twenty-three years died of brain cancer, Mouse, her Chihuahua, had brought her great comfort in the lonely weeks after her husband passed.

A year later, Barbara met a man with whom she fell in love. She moved into his house. And that's when the trouble began. The man told her that he didn't want to have a dog in his home. Barbara wrote, "In a moment of desperation and because I was trying to please this man, I took Mouse to the animal shelter. I would not have given up Mouse for any other person. When I returned home, he was angry about what I did because he felt guilty. I was heartbroken. The man had such mood swings that I thought [if I retrieved Mouse], he would change his mind, and I'd have to go through this again if he said Mouse had to go. Also, Mouse wasn't happy around the man. So I did not go back to get her from the animal shelter. The dog was a popular breed, and I hoped she would be adopted right away."

Later, Barbara realized that this man was very selfish and she ended her relationship with him. But Mouse was gone. She wrote, "I can still see that dog turning around to look at me when the intake person from the animal shelter took her away. I asked him to call me if they could not find a good home for Mouse. He said that they were not going to call. He advised that if I wanted to keep the dog, I should take her back now. I didn't check to see if Mouse had been adopted. Now, I live my life with regret over the decision to send Mouse away. I do not know what I was thinking back then." Barbara has been filled with remorse ever since. She phrased her desperation this way: "I need absolution and I don't know where to get it. I don't know how I could have been so stupid. How do I get rid of this pain?"[11]

When we published Barbara's letter in *Angel Animals Story of the Week*, readers from around the world came through with affirming and compassionate responses that may help ease your own burdens of guilt and regret.

Marty Tousley, a bereavement counselor, congratulated Barbara for having the courage to share her guilt about Mouse with the rest of the newsletter readers. Marty suggested that Mouse had, in a sense, given her life to protect Barbara. The dog had enabled Barbara to see what a selfish man she was involved with and how destructive their relationship was. She wrote, "Mouse became your guardian angel, and I'm sure she's somewhere out there watching over you still."[12]

In a situation similar to Barbara's, Carol gave up her two twelve-year-old cats. When she visited the University of Minnesota's Arboretum in Chanhassen, Carol was able to heal with the help of a wandering golden tabby who looked like one of her previous cats. Carol wrote, "The cat fearlessly sat in my lap in that cold autumn weather and let me hold and pet him for over an hour. I felt as if I was being given a blessing of love by this cat that allowed me to forgive myself."[13]

After the kindness and understanding our readers expressed,

Barbara wrote back to thank them. We published her letter in the next newsletter. She wrote, "I guess it's true that we usually punish ourselves far more than others would."[14]

In *Animals and the Afterlife*, author Kim Sheridan writes, "When guilt is justified, it's important to honor the guilt, learn from it, and vow to do things differently the next time we're faced with a similar situation. However, once we've acknowledged the guilt and truly learned from it, it's time to release the guilt and move forward. Usually there's a lesson in it so that we can make better decisions in the future, or else the tragedy is turned around by becoming a catalyst for something positive. We always get a chance to 'make things right' in the end."[15]

Following are ways to move beyond guilt, regret, and the need to keep trying to strike bargains with powers outside yourself.

1. FORGIVE YOURSELF. Remember how much you loved your animal companion. Know that you would never have done anything to hurt her. Think about what your pet would say to you and offer those words of forgiveness and compassion to yourself.

2. TALK ABOUT YOUR REGRETS AND GUILT WITH SOMEONE WHO WILL NOT JUDGE YOU. Choose your listeners carefully and let out all the pain, doubts, and confusion surrounding the loss until you start to realize that you did all you could or knew to do at the time.

3. WRITE ABOUT YOUR FEELINGS OF GUILT AND REGRET. Write to your pet and tell him that you're sorry for what you did or did not do for him. Tell your story. If you are

justified in having regrets, write a letter to a pet publication or a website that accepts such stories. Educate others with what you have learned and would do differently.

4. **GIVE YOURSELF THIRTY MINUTES OF SELF-JUDGMENT.** Rita Reynolds in *Blessing the Bridge* writes, "When I've laid my cards on the table, so to speak, I give myself exactly thirty minutes to sort them out. During this time I can berate myself, forgive myself, allow myself to be absolutely wretched and self-pitying. It is important to bring all those feelings up into the light. After that, it's time to let them go. If, after thirty minutes, I haven't completely resolved my guilt, I simply ask forgiveness of myself. Then, with as much calmness and clarity as possible, I turn within to my own center and ask for help and guidance."[16]

MEDITATION

Can you reflect upon the circumstances of your animal companion's death and forgive yourself? What would your pet say now that might make you feel better about your decisions?

Sadness and Depression

Robert Frost wrote in a poem about loss, "I have been one acquainted with the night."[17] Pet loss has acquainted many of us with the night. Your nights may be extending as you sleep a lot longer, or they may be torturous as you wrestle with insomnia. You may be eating too much or too little. A sense of hopelessness and despair could be making you feel listless, anxious, fearful, or despondent. The color blue in the rainbow may be washing over your life with overwhelming sadness.

Grieving over pet loss may be complicated by other losses you have endured, whether recently or in the past. Some people go through a series of losses simultaneously as chapters in their lives close in rapid succession. Often depression deepens if the lost pet was a link to someone who has previously left your life through death, separation, or divorce. Now you are mourning multiple losses, and it's difficult to comprehend that the ocean behind this wave of grief comes from something else.

Losses are also complicated when the death was violent, sudden, or accidental. Images of the dying animal may linger in your mind, causing nightmares or even post-traumatic stress disorder. These kinds of losses will probably require that you seek professional help from a bereavement counselor or therapist.

Sometimes it helps to remember the signs that your animal companion must have sensed death was imminent and even that she welcomed it as a relief from suffering. You may have, without realizing it, asked your pet if this was the right time for her to die. The answer may have come in ways you didn't recognize then but that can comfort and lift you out of despair now.

Often after you ask the animal if he is ready to die, he will do something uncharacteristic as a way of trying to communicate with you. Sometimes an animal who has been very sick will rally enough to make eye contact, reach out a paw to touch you, or show affection to you in a way that undeniably says he is saying goodbye. The animal may appear to you in a dream and give an answer through imagery, such as walking away from you until he disappears.

Don Marx asked his Maine Coon cat, Kit-3, to give him a clear sign that a fatal disease had run its course and it was time for the cat to leave this world. That night, after requesting an irrefutable sign, Don was surprised to find the cat walking toward him on his bed. For weeks, Kit-3 hadn't had the strength to jump on the bed. Don wrote, "Kit-3 stood staring down at me, lowered himself, and pressed his closed mouth against my lips for several seconds. Then he rested his head on my arm for a moment, and I kissed him again. He rose, made his way to the foot of the bed and onto the floor again. That, I knew, was the signal I had asked for. Kit-3 kissed me goodbye."

MEDITATION

Take a moment to remember signs that your animal companion gave to let you know the time of death was approaching.

Your grief is natural and understandable. It is what it is. But you know in your heart that this delightful soul, who shared your deepest joys and sorrows, would want for you to find happiness again.

Relief, Resignation, and Acceptance

Who knows when it will happen? You wake up one day and it doesn't hurt as much. You spend an entire hour or day not thinking about your loss. You walk a path you used to share with your best-friend animal or you see an animal who resembles yours, and you don't cry. Instead, a smile steals across your face. A happy memory drifts into your mind. A warm feeling sweeps over you.

During the acceptance phase of grieving, you may be relieved that your pet no longer has to suffer. There might be things you can do now that you weren't able to do while your pet was ill. Yet relief, as normal as it is, can lead to another wave of guilt. So you berate yourself for enjoying a day without the creature who lit up your life with his presence. You wonder if you are coldhearted because you slept through the night without dreaming of him or missing him snuggling near you in the bed.

Life is carrying you forward on a wave of acceptance.

TRY THIS EXERCISE

Reread the headings for the phases of grief. See if you can identify where you are on the continuum of grieving and healing. Write about how aspects of this element of grieving are affecting you, your relationships, and your daily living.

Organic grieving, like an unexpected intruder, may surprise you with its presence, because the various aspects of grief can pop up without warning. In her wonderfully practical book *Bouncing Back*, the comedian Joan Rivers writes about grief: "Whether it hits you weeks or months after your loss, the second wave of grief can make you wonder if you're allowed to call yourself a survivor. It can make you wonder if your life will ever be normal."[18]

By allowing yourself to grieve organically, at your own pace and in your own individual way, accepting what you're thinking and feeling becomes easier, and the pain gradually subsides. Rainbow blue is replaced by your growing capacity for reconciling the past with the present and the future. Then it will be helpful to remember what you have lost. The red light of remembrance brings buried grief and unexpressed pain to the surface, so healing will continue.

Now, let us remember.

MEDITATION

Anger and Forgiveness

I acknowledge all of my feelings and accept that they are natural expressions of the grief over losing you.

I am angry about what caused you to die.

I want to shake my fist or scream at the caregivers who did not save your life.

I am angry with God for taking you away too soon.

It upsets me that you left this world even though I still needed you.

What can I say or think or do to forgive myself or others for not being able to stop you from dying?

MEDITATION

The Effects of Grief

You were an important part of my life, and I feel an overpowering grief and sadness over your loss. My life is affected in simple and profound ways. I am hurting emotionally, physically, and mentally. I am often distracted and unfocused during my regular workday. My sadness over missing you leaves me numb and unmotivated.

- What are the things that I miss the most, now that you are gone?
- What are my thoughts and feelings as I try to perform daily activities?
- What are the responsibilities and items on my to-do list that I can put on the back burner while my attention is diverted by your death?

CHAPTER TWO

Rainbow Red
Remembering the Life of Your Angel Animal

I know you by heart. You are inside my heart.
— Frances Hodgson Burnett, *A Little Princess*

Long waves in a shaft of sunlight transform inside raindrops and create the color red on a rainbow's outer rim. We like to think of the color red as a symbol for remembering. Just as a crimson fire can emit warmth even after its flames have died down, red hot memories of your angel animal will help you continue to feel the glow of his or her presence. Oddly enough, the more you let yourself remember the days you spent together, the easier it ultimately is to let go and accept that those days are gone but not forgotten. The red of memory comforts long after your beloved pet's death.

Why remember?

Because remembering honors. Remembering heals. Remembering forgives. Remembering creates appreciation and gratitude — two of the most wondrous salves for your sorrows.

People sometimes think that they will feel better by denying their grief and refusing to remember what has caused it. In some cases and at certain times, that may be true. As your life continues to demand that you support yourself, care for others, and be out and about in the world, you may need to place your memories on hold. But grief is like a bill collector: you can delay facing it, but if you do so for too long, it will come to meet you at your front door. Grief will have its day, whether you consciously allow it to or not. So it is in your best interest to heal the wounds of grief with remembrance.

Refusing to remember can cause bitterness, pain, and anger to appear to fade away. But buried grief lies in wait and pounces unexpectedly. Buried grief casts an invisible veil of sadness over every future relationship. It whispers that to love means to suffer. It convinces you that life offers nothing but despair. The dammed-up river of unresolved grief makes it easier for each subsequent loss to burst through your defenses.

With organic grieving, you will not bury your grief. Instead, you will allow the rhythms of your emotions to ebb and flow naturally. By giving yourself the gift of remembering your animal companion, grief will seep back into and enrich the soil of your life instead of creating poisonous wells of unresolved sadness inside you.

WHO WAS THIS ANIMAL TO YOU?

Taking the time and effort to remember details about your pet will help you to understand the important roles she played in your life. J. Allen Boone, in his classic book *Kinship with All Life*, recalls his relationship with the dog Strongheart, who became known as Rin Tin Tin. What Boone says about dogs can be applied to any animal who has shared your home: "Sooner or later the observant human comes to discover that practically every dog is innately equipped with valuable knowledge and wisdom and is a master in the art of teaching humans by means of the irresistible power of a silent good example."[1]

TRY THIS EXERCISE

Stop now and remember how it felt to share your life with a special partner who:

- Never betrayed you
- Loved you even when you were having a bad day
- Didn't have to be the one who got in the last word
- Treated you as the child she was determined to parent
- Didn't get huffy when you used baby talk with him
- May have been your last link to someone else you love or miss
- Offered protection, security, or physical service
- Didn't judge you, and yet immediately forgave you

- Became your silent best friend and confidant
- Treated you better than any lover or spouse did
- Showed you love, compassion, and wisdom

In the poem "Request from the Rainbow Bridge," Constance Jenkins wrote in loving memory of her dog, Isolde Jenkins, "Remember not my fight for breath / Remember not the strife. / Please do not dwell upon my death, / But celebrate my life."[2]

Remembering will bring you to a place where you can willingly and easily celebrate the life of an animal who meant so much to you. For Sheryl Jordan, an act of remembrance helped her heal from the grief of losing her mother and, shortly afterward, her two dogs, Missy and Sparky. Sheryl wrote to us about an important healing memory. She asked her deceased mother to send a yellow rose (her mother's favorite kind) as an assurance that she still was watching over her daughter. Within a few weeks, a little yellow kitten came running out of the woods where Sheryl had always walked her dogs. This kitten showed no fear. Sheryl picked her up, and the kitten purred a happy hello. She named the kitten Pumpkin.

The odd part of this story is that Sheryl lives on an island with only one bridge to the main road. It seemed impossible for the kitten to have suddenly appeared in Sheryl's woods.

One night, Sheryl lay in bed, sobbing and grieving over the triple loss of her mother and the two dogs. She wrote, "My heart was breaking. I was in physical pain. Little Pumpkin hopped into bed with me and laid her paw on my heart. She kept it there for over an hour as I sobbed and drifted off to sleep. It seemed as if she knew the pain was in my heart and tried to comfort me there."

As if to make sure that Sheryl knew that remembering her mother and the deceased dogs was important for helping her to heal, Pumpkin continued her role of comforting angel. One day, while Sheryl was working at her desk, tears overcame her again. She wrote, "Pumpkin came from somewhere in my house. She laid her paw on my shoulder and again, kept it there. She then crawled into my lap, laid both of her paws on my chest, and looked deeply into my eyes."

After this second act of compassion, Sheryl finally got the message. She had asked for a yellow rose as a sign to remind her of her mother's continued spiritual presence. She realized that yellow-colored Pumpkin was her mother's sign. She renamed the kitten Rose.[3]

THE DAY YOU MET

Do you remember when you first met this creature who transformed you into a better human being? Did you have déjà vu when you and your animal companion connected? Many people feel as if they are renewing old acquaintances with their new pet. Christine Davis, in *For Every Dog an Angel*, writes, "From time to time, when a certain person and a certain dog meet, something happens that is just like magic! It is as if they have known each other before."[4]

Did you choose your animal companion? Did he choose you? Or was the choosing mutual?

We have received hundreds of letters and stories from people who are convinced that the animal did as much or more of the choosing as they did. Armida Turk wrote about the battle-scarred black cat with fleas, ear mites, broken teeth, and an upper respiratory infection who wandered out of the northern Minnesota woods and chose to become her new companion and partner in the work of rescuing other animals:

He was wary and afraid of humans. I put food out for him every day for six months before he came close and let me touch him. It seemed he had been longing for the caresses of human hands all along, because when he finally let me pet him, his back came up to meet my hand.

Why he was a stray will forever remain a mystery. I do believe someone must have loved him before me because Scruffy (as I named him) was so lovable and a very well behaved house cat. He neither went anywhere near an open door nor made any indication that he wanted to go back outside.

This raggedy-looking old cat, an angel in disguise no doubt, nurtured and played with the many orphaned kittens I fostered for the local animal shelter, Friends of Animals. He would anchor a rambunctious, squirming kitten to the floor with his powerful fore-leg then tenderly give him a bath as lovingly and gently as any mother cat.

Scruffy was happy and playful even at his advanced age, which was estimated to be eight to ten years at the time he entered my life. That is old for a cat living on his own outdoors. His favorite toy was a small wad of paper that he batted around the floor at blinding speeds. He knew the whir of an electric can opener was often synonymous with some cat delight. He would awaken from a seemingly sound sleep and race into the kitchen to see if I had anything for him. He loved popcorn, chips, and most any people snack food.

MEDITATION

What significant details do you remember about how you met your special animal? Why do you think this animal came into your life at the time he or she did?

DAILY-LIFE MEMORIES

Details are important. The details of remembrance will become stepping-stones across your stream of grief. As you write or talk to a trusted friend about an animal companion's unique personality, intelligence, quirks, and qualities, remember the highs and lows of your relationship as vividly as you can. Were there certain incidents with your beloved pet that still stand out, even years later?

In organic grieving, you accept that whatever memories float to the surface are worthy of your attention, no matter how trivial they may seem to be. The daily routines and rituals you shared with your animal companion will be exactly what you need to cherish his memory and restore yourself.

Pamela Jenkins gives a beautiful example of remembering daily-life details as a way of healing. She writes about her deceased dog: "I miss the walks I used to have with Tyrel. He was a lot of fun, didn't pull on the leash, and he'd stop to smell the roses with me. Well, he'd stop to smell, anyway. Each outing was an adventure to him. With a bounce in his step and dancing eyes, he'd look up at me as if to say, 'Now, aren't we having fun?'

"Since Ty passed on, I've missed the daily escape to the outdoors. I've been without a dog to walk. The thing I used to enjoy has lost much of its appeal. Outings aren't nearly as refreshing. The great outdoors aren't quite so 'great' anymore. Time to get back in the habit."[5]

TRY THIS EXERCISE

Make a list of the enjoyable habits and routines you shared with your animal companion. Next to each item, write whether you think you can resume or modify the activity now. If the activity is still too painful for you to do again, just write, "Not ready yet." Eventually, you may find that going back to a shared routine brings comfort as you remember the joy of doing it together with your animal partner.

PRIOR TO THE PASSING

Some of your most painful memories may revolve around those days and nights before your precious pet left you. Perhaps you provided hospice care for the animal when he was sick but not ready to die. Remembering all you did to make those waning times as peaceful and free of suffering as possible will ease the burdens of guilt and regret you may be feeling.

After the vet said he could do nothing more for Buffy, Mary Elizabeth Martucci decided to care for her invalid cat, a companion who had given her many years of unconditional love and pleasure. Mary wrote of the daily routines that made Buffy's remaining days comfortable:

> I fed Buffy antibiotics, cortisone, water by dropper, and baby food. I bathed her, placed her in bed (fortified with plastic underpads), and changed her position throughout the day. At times, Buffy would reach out and touch me, seemingly asking for me not to give up on her. After the first week of my caring for her with such meticulousness, Buffy gained more strength. She swallowed food easier, drank water from a paper cup, and pulled herself to a sitting position without help. Remarkably, she seemed hungry, so I added to her diet and by week's end, she was also eating dry food.
>
> Soon, Buffy had the routines down pat and even cooperated in her care. After breakfast, which Buffy now ate with little aid, I bathed her. Buffy turned with little assistance, resting her head on a towel as I dried and brushed her fur. Passive exercises to her hind legs provided stimulation. The most unique behavior my remarkable cat displayed, though, was her response to my saying, "It's time to poo." Buffy's paralyzed legs would quiver, and then move back and forth. I'd place a Styrofoam cup under her tail as I lifted her hindquarters, and she'd drop the stool directly into the cup! Amazing? It was to me!
>
> On sunny days, I placed Buffy's bed on her window seat. She enjoyed watching her animal friends at play outdoors. Buffy liked

to be carried in her bed to different rooms where once she had free rein. When I spoke to her, Buffy sat up and looked at me, seeming to understand. If I told her to "sleep until I return," she positioned herself in bed and did just that. Occasionally she uttered a soft meow in response but always, her large, pale, yellow eyes told me what she wanted.

How did you prepare yourself and your pet for the time when she would be waiting for you at the Rainbow Bridge? Bringing to mind the period of time just prior to your pet's passing may be painful at first, but it can contribute greatly to reassurance that you did whatever love inspired you to do.

REMEMBERING THE MOMENT OF DEATH

The philosopher and ethicist Martin Buber wrote, "Death constitutes the final limit of all that we are able to imagine."[6] If you were present for your animal companion's death, you may have walked with him to the gates, but you could not accompany him through. Now that your animal friend is gone, imagination may be failing you, because you're uncertain about what lies beyond, even as you visualize your pet at the Rainbow Bridge. Remembering the ending of your pet's life, recalling what you experienced outwardly and inwardly, will bring back the sorrow of loss. But it also can remind you that it is an honor to be present at the closing moments of a well-lived life. If you didn't witness your pet's dying but someone else was there, now would be a good time to ask for that person's impressions of the event. Of course, not all deaths are peaceful. But even those animals who die tragically have left their bodies for an existence that is free of pain.

As you remember the moment of death, try not to doubt yourself or your perceptions. Many people have witnessed the soul, spirit, or a light leaving the animal's body at the moment of death. They report seeing the animal's light-body leaping to freedom from a physical shell that could no longer hold such a great spirit.

People often tell us that remembering the moment of death makes them feel peaceful. Jenni Dewar chose to be with her cat Mouser, who had been her faithful friend throughout her teenage years, when Jenni had struggled with clinical depression. She wrote about taking Mouser for his last visit to the vet, after his diagnosis of fatal cancer: "Mouser was very peaceful. I held him as the vet shaved his arm and put the needle in his vein. Most people don't understand why I wanted to be in the room while Mouser died, but I would never have left him to go alone, just as he never left me during difficult times. As it turns out, it was a wonderful experience. When Mouser left, I felt his soul go through me and I clearly heard him thank me for letting him go. I felt such peace and happiness in that moment that I knew I had made the right decision. I was reassured that Mouser loved me just as much as I loved him. I know I will see him again and that he is at peace."

TRY THIS EXERCISE

Many people are honored to be present as their animal friend leaves the physical body. Have the courage now to remember what it was like to be there. This memory may become one of your greatest healing agents. If you weren't present, imagine your animal companion's release from life to death to life without pain.

One of the reasons people treasure the memory of being present at the moment of death is that the animal may have faced it with remarkable courage and dignity. Witnessing death often causes a person to realize that dying is a transition from one form to another, not a final ending. The animals can teach all of us much about death and dying. Michele F. Edgcomb wrote to us about her cat Lily:

Lily was always a very fearful cat. Fear dominated her life and kept her prisoner within the house. Lily hid from strangers, from certain sounds, even from me at times. Knowing she had to see the vet, I was concerned about how she would react. Never having been ill, Lily had seldom been to the vet's office. I was relieved when she seemed to become at ease. Later the same day, she went to the emergency clinic for hospitalization. I was allowed to visit her and was astonished to see how calm she was. As I spoke to Lily, she would look past me to watch the doctors and staff. Their activity fascinated her. She actually welcomed their affectionate attentions, and when they examined or handled her, she was perfectly at ease.

I realized that somehow, sometime, Lily had managed to cast off the fears of a lifetime. In doing so, she was prepared to face death with the inner peace that insures a fluid transition. Lily accepted her fate bravely and was truly serene in her final hours. I was so proud of her. Her acceptance was a profound comfort to me. Because she did not resist death, I didn't either. It hurts yet, but I am so happy for her that the most unfamiliar and intimidating journey was the easiest. We can all learn from Lily. Few of us will attain her spiritual serenity, but what a fine thing to aspire to.

MEDITATION

What has an animal taught you about dying and the moment of death?

HOW TO REMEMBER YOUR ANIMAL COMPANION'S DEATH

You can mourn your loss as Christina Louise Dicker did, by writing about what you miss the most. Christina wrote, "Sylvester was an amazing creature. He was nine years of age when he left us. We miss his noisy purring and his even noisier snoring. We miss the touch of his big, pink nose and the connection with those soulful, sparkling eyes. But his memory will never fade. We buried Sylvester's beautiful body beneath a tribute tree, but his invincible spirit lives on in our happy home."

TRY THIS EXERCISE

Write or talk about what you recall of the moment of your pet's death and the time just prior to it. Assemble photos of your animal companion in good health and look at them. Allow yourself to remember the funny, sad, miraculous,

touching, irritating, and joyful details of your pet's life and
death.

MEDITATION

How We Chose Each Other

You came into my life in a way that unmistakably told
me to bring you home. But I think we chose each other.
This was one of the best decisions I ever made.

- What did you see in me that made you want to be
  my friend?
- Did we have a sacred agreement to be together?
- What were we supposed to give to and receive from
  each other?
- Did we complete our contract of love?
- What can I learn from our choices to be together
  that will help me with other relationships?

From the Appendix, you may want to use the additional meditations "I Remember You," "The Courage to Remember," and
"Memories of Daily Life" to extend the consolation you can receive by lovingly reliving meaningful times from the past.

MEDITATION

How We Missed Each Other

When we left our home together, you had things you liked and did not like about being away. When I left on my own, there were things you disliked about my being gone.

I remember how you showed me what you felt when I left the house.

I remember how you greeted me when I returned home.

We spent fun and playful times together. I remember the games and activities that amused you and made me laugh.

There are so many things I miss about you and the life we shared. Today, most of all, I miss:_____.

CHAPTER THREE

Rainbow Yellow
The Spirituality of an Angel Animal's Death

Think of him faring on, as dear
In the love of There as the love of Here.
Think of him still as the same. I say,
He is not dead — he is just away.

— James Whitcomb Riley, "He Is Not Dead"

Now we turn our gaze to yellow, the golden hue in the rainbow. It is time to mine the spiritual treasures that you have received from the soul in an animal's body who blessed your life with his presence.

No one sees exactly the same rainbow. Standing in different places with their backs to the sun, two people experience the rainbow's colors in ways that are uniquely their own. In a symbolic sense, this is especially true of rainbow yellow. It is the spiritually significant color that reminds you of your beliefs about what lies beyond the border of death.

Everyone has his or her own beliefs about divinity, death, and whether or not animals have souls, and these beliefs may or may not jibe with the teachings of religious leaders and theologians. Alan D. Wolfelt touched on this dichotomy in his book *When Your Pet Dies*: "Now I'm not a theologian, and I know that various organized religions weigh in differently on this matter, but as a pet lover I can tell you that my dogs had souls and I expect to see them again one day. When it comes to this matter, listen to your heart."[1]

A bit less definite, Wallace Sife nevertheless is willing to consider that animals have souls. He writes, "There is nothing in scripture that suggests any living thing other than man has a soul. To wonder about this is a projection of our anthropomorphic fantasy; we are limited to our human perspective. But it must also be said that there is nothing in the scriptures that denies the existence of a soul for any other creature of creation. We are just not privy to God's larger view of truth. One could assume that there is some spiritual dimension to the life and death of other forms in God's creation. But that would be a personal assumption."[2]

Some people believe that animals come from, and return at death to, a group spirit, or oversoul. Others beg to differ. The veterinarian Martin Goldstein says, "Having lived and worked with so many dogs and cats, getting to know them as well as I have, and hearing so many accounts of their return, I believe that animals definitely have individual spirits. Are their spirits like ours? I think they're less complex. Humans have greater intelligence; the power of the animal spirit is its simplicity. We make ourselves miserable with our fear of death, and have an almost constitutional inability to live in the moment. Our pets have no vices. They love without qualification, exhibit loyalty and courage, have no fear of death, and live every moment fully for itself. Who's purer?"[3]

TRY THIS EXERCISE

Write what you truly believe about animals in relation to your beliefs about the soul, death, and the afterlife. Reread what you wrote. If you find portions that repeat what you have been taught versus what you have experienced, underline those parts in a different color. Let this writing exercise sit for a while. Don't try to change your beliefs, but allow yourself the freedom not to debate or doubt them for now.

Later, you may find that your beliefs are reaffirmed, or that they are re-arranging themselves. Now that your animal companion has left this physical world, you have had a firsthand experience with death and dying. Continue to write about any confusion without the expectation that you'll immediately have all the answers to your questions. In other words, give yourself permission to float along with the waves of change that death inevitably creates.

OUR PERSONAL BELIEFS ABOUT
ANIMALS, SOULS, AND DEATH

We want to share with you what we believe about animals, souls, death, dying, the afterlife, and reincarnation. As with everyone else's opinions, what matters the most for you is what you believe. We base our beliefs on our personal experiences with people, animals, and spiritual study, as well as on the thousands of letters and stories we've received over the years from people who have had visits, visions, dreams, assistance from the other side, and the return of an animal through reincarnation.

We believe that animals don't have a soul. Animals are souls. We believe that animals and humans are cut from the same divine cloth by the same divine hand. As souls, we are all one; we are all interconnected. Each soul experiences life in whatever way serves it best spiritually in this lifetime. As individual sparks of God, or the Divine, you and your animal companions are one-of-a-kind souls, learning about life, expanding your consciousness, and growing (or regressing) depending on how profoundly you love. (Notice we didn't say depending on how smart you are.) All souls grow spiritually in the sweet garden of unconditional love — an aspect of life in which animals tend to excel. Animals are masters at loving as God loves, unconditionally. We like the viewpoint of the biochemist and philosopher Rupert Sheldrake, who writes in *Dogs That Know When Their Owners Are Coming Home*, "One of the most consistent features of accounts of the comforting and healing behavior of companion animals is that they respond to people's needs. They are not simply behaving in a generically affectionate manner."[4]

Before birth, as souls, you and your animal companion make a sacred agreement to teach and to learn from each other. In order for the two souls to keep these contracts of love, each has to come into this world at exactly the right time and in exactly the right form to connect with the other. There are no mistakes at the Divine train station. Souls arrive and leave on time and make it to their destinations with sacred precision.

The soul that becomes a dog, cat, iguana, bird, rabbit, goldfish, hamster, or horse took on the necessary body and was born at the necessary time to keep his or her appointment with destiny. As souls, animals and people set up certain signals so that they will recognize one another and know it is the right time to be reunited. Signals such as, "I'll be in this animal shelter on this date. I'll be waiting there for you. Don't be late."

How well people carry out the spiritual assignments that they and their animal companion agree to is a matter of free will. But as souls, humans and animals make a pact to meet, to live together, and to be catalysts for one another in this spiritual classroom known as earth.

When the animal and person die, it may not be the end of their journey together. Each soul takes a new path and a different form after shedding its physical body. They may reunite after death when they meet in a heavenly plane. If it is best for both of them spiritually, the souls could reincarnate together. Or, since an animal's lifespan is shorter than his human friend's, a person's childhood pet may come back as a new animal friend in his or her adulthood.

The soul never dies. As long as the bond of love remains between two souls, they will be together, and the love they share will always be their greatest teacher.

MEDITATION

What do you believe? What spiritual points of view make sense to you? What is the death of your beloved pet teaching you about heaven, animals as souls, and spiritual growth?

YELLOW IS THE SPIRITUAL NATURE OF ANIMALS AT DEATH

Whether you believe that animals are or have souls, you probably would agree that they show spiritual qualities we humans long to have more of in our lives. Without committing the "sin" of anthropomorphism, most of us have noticed that animals exhibit the spiritual awareness to live in the present, love without expecting a return, and offer compassion to humans and to other animals. Shirley MacLaine, in her book *Out on a Leash*, writes alternately from her own perspective and from that of her dog, Terry. In one section of the book Terry "writes": "I'm always in touch with the light inside myself. Holding on to worries just blocks your view of the light inside of you."[5] Wise words, indeed, from a soul wearing a doggie body!

At an animal's death, many humans get a glimpse of the animal's relationship with Spirit. Some people notice the animal looking at something that is invisible to humans, even seeming to communicate with it. They wonder, Could the animal be seeing an angel? Others witness a white light or a lighter version of the animal leaving his physical body at the moment of death. Whether or not you saw a spiritual presence, if you were there at the time of your animal companion's death, you may have sensed a soul leaving its physical shell.

MEDITATION

In the classic children's novel *A Little Princess*, Frances Hodgson Burnett writes, "How it is that animals understand things I do not know, but it is certain that they do understand. Perhaps there is a language which is not made of words and everything in the world understands it. Perhaps there is a soul hidden in everything and it can always speak, without even making a sound, to another soul."[6]

What is an animal soul trying to say to you as you read this chapter and reflect upon its messages?

PRANA'S CONTRACT OF LOVE

We're compelled to give one more example of the color yellow, which signifies the spiritual connection between people and animals that reunites them at the Rainbow Bridge. There are profoundly sacred agreements that two souls, wearing the physical bodies of different species, can keep with each other. Perhaps the following story of Allen and our dog Prana's healing nature will remind you of your own divine covenants with the animals who have shared your life and continue to love you, even after death.

During what now seems like a past lifetime, in the 1980s, I worked as a police officer on a city beat where violence was the rule rather than the exception. Because I was assigned to the evening shift, I would arrive home near midnight. Usually Linda and our children were already asleep. This meant that the sole greeter was our golden retriever, Prana. She would welcome me with tail wagging and doggie kisses. After changing out of my uniform, I'd sit on the floor with her and feel the stress from work dissipating. As if this was her job and she had agreed to perform it to perfection, Prana became my constant source of emotional healing.

One night, though, I was reminded of how carefully Prana was taking care of me, when I arrived home feeling exceptionally stressed out. In addition to answering an unusually large number of calls, I had witnessed two unnerving acts of domestic violence. While apprehending a brutal criminal, I'd had to stop myself from becoming his judge and jury instead of only the arresting officer. Fortunately I managed to get control of my emotions, but their strength had left me shaken and exhausted. I could hardly wait to get home and shut out a world where I was being forced to have close and personal experiences with the worst in human nature.

From the moment I came in the door, Prana seemed to sense that I needed something different from her. Instead of her usual exuberant greeting that night, she walked over and nuzzled my leg with her nose and waited to be petted. Linda had left a lamp on in the living room. I walked to sit on the sofa but felt myself slumping down to the floor. Feelings of devastation and hopelessness swept through my body. That's when Prana really went to work.

This gentle dog placed her paws on my legs and pressed her head against my heart. I put my arms around her and held her close, feeling love pouring into me from every fiber of her being. She made me feel that I was home, and that the creatures I loved most on this earth would sustain me through these turbulent times.

Later, when I left police work and moved my family to Minnesota and began employment in a much more tranquil job and environment, Prana continued to be my healing companion. But the years took their toll, and Prana became ill. Facing her death was one of the hardest things I've ever had to do.

Even as she neared the end, Prana made it clear that her desire to serve by giving love took precedence over her own needs. When the vet called to tell us that the surgery to remove Prana's cancer had been unsuccessful, his voice cracked as he conveyed what else he had found. He said that in a most unusual way, it seemed as if Prana had done more than was possible to stay alive. Her intestinal wall had started to grow new, healthy tissue around one of the tumors. But the cancer had already taken over too much of her body, and she couldn't heal. Painfully, I had to consent to having my beloved companion euthanized to end her suffering. All of her life, she had healed me, and now I had to let her go to a heavenly home where she could heal.

Does the contract of love between Allen and Prana bring to mind your own sacred agreements with animals who have blessed your life with their presence? Was there some deeper level of spiritual connection that now comforts you with the certainty that you will be with each other again?

In the next part of this book, we'll look at the bridges of support, comfort, and shelter that can offer what you need as you continue your journey through grieving over the loss of your pet.

MEDITATION

Ask the Divine

I ask God, the Divine, the Holy Spirit, Jesus, one of the heavenly protectors of animals, or my guardian angels to guide me to a spiritual connection with you.

I fill my heart with love and visualize you.

I ask whatever questions I want answered now.

- As I write down all of the thoughts, impressions, and images that come into my mind and touch my heart, what questions are you answering?
- How can I reflect on what I have received in a way that helps me today?

MEDITATION

I Feel You Near Me

At times, I continue to feel your presence nearby. This is how I feel when I sense that you are with me spiritually:_____.

There are times when I feel that I am entering a higher state of consciousness to gain insight into our spiritual relationship.

This is what I feel about those experiences:_____.

My beliefs about the two of us being together again after my death are:_____.

Bridges
Crossing Over the River of Grief Together

*It was wholly unreasonable to me — this was even before
I had gone to school — that in my evening devotions
I should pray only for me. So when my mother had prayed
with me and kissed me goodnight, I used secretly to add
another prayer which I had myself composed for all living
creatures. It ran like this: "Dear God, guard and bless everything that
breathes; keep it from all evil and give it quiet sleep."*

— Albert Schweitzer, "A Prayer for All Living Creatures"

CHAPTER FOUR

Covered Bridges
Shelters from the Storms of Pet Loss

Where many were, but few remain
Of old familiar things,
But seeing them to mind again
The lost and absent brings.

— Abraham Lincoln, "Memory"

S ince ancient times, bridges have enabled people to cross over obstacles that were considered impassable. Bridges have connected people of differing cultures and customs. They have allowed for commerce and the exchange of ideas. Bridges have become symbols of unity.

The Rainbow Bridge stretches across the expanse between life and death. In the story, the bridge is said to link heaven and earth. Your animal companion, who has gone before you, waits at the Rainbow Bridge. After you have greeted each other, you will walk together to the other side, where your forever friendship will be celebrated and honored.

This chapter focuses on a type of bridge that evokes romantic images of a quieter, simpler time. The covered bridge, also known as the "kissing bridge," emerged in the eighteenth century out of necessity. Swollen creeks and rivers made efficient transportation across many parts of the American landscape impossible. Since wood was the most widely available material for building bridges, and it easily succumbed to bad weather conditions, covers were devised to protect the bridge structures. Soon, covered bridges became protectors of travelers trying to escape storms and of lovers seeking private places for exchanging kisses.

Your human and animal family, sympathetic friends, and even strangers may become the covered bridges that help you weather the storms of loneliness and shock after the loss of an animal companion.

FAMILY AND FRIENDS

In her book *Bouncing Back*, Joan Rivers offers sage advice for letting others know that you still need their understanding. She writes, "If you aren't getting the support you need, speak up and spell things out for both friends and acquaintances. Eager to return to their lives after helping you, your friends can lose track of your continuing pain, especially after a formal period of mourning. Don't be shy about working updates on how you're feeling into the conversation."[1]

The people closest to you can be your most reliable or your leakiest covered bridges. Anyone who trivializes or dismisses your grief with statements such as "It was only an animal" doesn't have a clue about what you're feeling. Worse, these kinds of remarks can make you feel even sadder and angrier. If you had to choose euthanasia for your pet, some people, upon learning of your decision, can become judgmental and unforgiving. *A good general rule to follow is, avoid people, places, and situations that make you feel worse instead of better.*

There's no need to put on a brave front if that's not how you're honestly feeling. Although you probably don't want to be crying in public or at work, if it happens, it happens. The afternoon that Prana died, we each took a personal day off from work, put our arms around each other, and walked out of the building, weeping openly. We went home and cried and consoled each other for the rest of the day.

Not every employer would be as understanding as ours were. In *Pet Loss*, Julia Harris writes, "People often wonder how they can introduce pet death to their employers when their grief is excessive and they need a day or two away from work to make suitable arrangements and calm down from the initial shock and emotional turmoil. Simply tell your employer that there has been a death in your immediate family. This is the truth. If your employer were to know that the departed one was your pet, he or she might not be so compassionate. Don't provide details or excuses. If asked who died, simply state that you are too upset to talk about it. You do not have to reveal any facts. Be assertive, but not confrontational. If you are denied the time off, at least you tried. More than likely your employer will grant you a day or two."[2]

TRY THIS EXERCISE

Make a list of things that people can say or do that you believe are or are not helpful in the phase of grieving you are
going through now. Share this list with trusted friends and
family members. For example, your list could include some
of the items below.

What You Can Say or Do
to Help Me Grieve and Recover

- Tell me you are sorry about my loss and that you understand my feelings run deep.
- Offer to help me care for my other pets for a while.
  Take over those responsibilities that remind me of my
  loss. Help me out with errands and other aspects of
  daily life, such as grocery shopping.
- Listen to me without making any judgments about my
  decisions.
- Join me in a memorial service for my pet and talk about
  your fondest memories of him.

What You Can Say or Do
That Makes Me Feel Worse about My Loss

- Discount or trivialize how deep and real my feelings of
  loss and anguish are and tell me to just get over it or to
  replace the pet who has died.

- Tell me that I should be glad I have one less thing to worry about or to drain me financially.
- Tell me your own stories of pet or human loss in a way that makes me feel you're trying to top mine.
- Say, "It's God's will," "God needed your pet in heaven," "You'll feel better in the morning," or any other such clichés.

Also, you may want to use the "Friends and Family" meditation in the Appendix as a way of bringing people close to you together for helping to say goodbye to your angel animal.

SEEKING PROFESSIONAL, ONLINE, OR GROUP SUPPORT

Your grief may be sliding into clinical depression or even thoughts of suicide, especially if your pet has played the role of your best friend, your child, or your main physical and emotional support system. Alan D. Wolfelt writes, "If you suspect you are clinically depressed, it is critically important that you take steps to get help."[3]

If you're experiencing intense and prolonged feelings of hopelessness, emptiness, sadness, shock, guilt, denial, or anxiety, it's a good idea to find a professional therapist who specializes in pet loss. Two questions to ask when you're looking for a therapist or counselor are: Have you ever had a pet die? and How did you feel when that happened? Check in with yourself as you listen to the therapist's responses. If he or she can't relate to the depth of emotion and suffering around this kind of loss, keep shopping around for one who will. In the Resources section of this book, you'll find listings of websites and hotlines that offer help from people who are sympathetic to the needs of people who have lost a pet.

If you're feeling sad but not clinically depressed, you may find that joining a local or online pet-loss support group will help you to find strangers who understand what you are feeling better than your friends and family do. Recommendations for such websites are in the Resources section. A word of caution, though: You're very vulnerable right now. Take care of yourself. If you find that a group or group members make you feel worse instead of better, drop out and find another that is more suited to your needs. Not all pet-loss groups are moderated by trained professionals. Volunteer leaders may not be skilled at keeping the group on track or stopping participants from saying hurtful or insensitive things. Be persistent in finding a group that is right for you.

CONSOLING THE SURVIVING ANIMALS IN A MULTIPLE-PET FAMILY

In *Learning Their Language*, the animal communicator and biologist Marta Williams writes, "When an animal dies, the surviving animals in the household and other animal friends may become just as emotionally devastated as the grieving people. While they do have the awareness that their friend can return, they also know

[that] when he does, . . . he will not be the same and he might not return for some time."[4]

Our two cockatiels, Sunshine and Sparkle, loved each other intensely. They were constant companions who occupied the same spacious cage, groomed each other's feathers, and irritated each other when cabin fever set in. One morning, after many bouts of illness, medications, and vet visits, we found Sparkle dead at the bottom of the cage. We watched helplessly as her devoted mate, Sunshine, walked in circles around her lifeless body. The bird keened with a mournful sound that we'd never heard before, nor has he repeated it since her death. For hours, Sunshine did his funeral ritual, stopping to nudge Sparkle with his beak as if he needed to convince himself that she was really dead.

We wondered when we should remove Sparkle from the cage and decided to take our cues from Sunshine. After about eight hours of his vigil, he finally left her side, climbed the ladder to his perch, and continued to look down at his dear friend. We asked Sunshine if he was ready for us to take Sparkle outside for her burial and memorial service. He turned his head away from us and from her, as if to say, "Go ahead. I know that she is gone now."

For many weeks, we gave Sunshine extra attention by singing and whistling to him often. Twice daily, we took him to the mantel, where he and Sparkle used to eat out of their seed bowl and groom each other. He would walk to the end of it and stare sadly out the window, as if looking for her return. After a couple of weeks, he began again to sing and whistle back to us. The day he flew from the mantel for his customary ride on Linda's shoulder while she prepared breakfast, we knew things were returning to some semblance of normalcy.

All through Sunshine's mourning period, we spoke to him of Sparkle. We talked about how special and pretty she was. We assured him that she had loved him in life and continued to love him after death. But he probably didn't need our words. We often observed him looking past us or cocking his head and following the flight of his invisible mate. We sensed that her spirit would stay nearby until she was certain that Sunshine could handle having her leave him.

After the death of a pet, it's natural for you to want to reach out to the other animals in your family as they mourn their dear companions. Rita Reynolds, founder of Howling Success, an animal sanctuary in Virginia, writes in *Blessing the Bridge*, "Time and again I have seen animals feel loss when another leaves, the pain sometimes so intense that it results in a serious illness, or even their own death. Animals feel the void left in the wake of death.... Therefore, it is vital to take such grieving creatures right on through the resolution process."[5]

Pet-loss books mention that the surviving pet may show signs of grieving by losing her appetite, becoming unusually aggressive or withdrawn, crying, moaning, or even becoming physically ill. Following are some of the most prevalent suggestions we've found in our research to help you help a surviving pet through the mourning period.

- Don't change the surviving pet's daily routines or diet. Try to keep everything as normal as possible.

- Be careful not to reward excessive depression or inactivity with extra attention. Instead, give your surviving pet lots of attention and affection when he is playing, exercising, and being active.
- Let survivors in a multiple-pet household work out their own issues about who is going to be in charge now and what the "pecking order" will be.

From our story about Sunshine and Sparkle, you can tell that we think it's important to let the surviving pet take as much time as he needs to say goodbye in his own way. Although not everyone accepts that animals understand human speech, we believe that they do. Almost always, we've noticed changes in behavior after having "discussions" with our animal companions. Reynolds writes, "I never hesitate to speak with the other animals in the family in a direct and honest manner, forming the clearest images I can."[6]

If your pet has been euthanized or was killed in an accident, visualize the process of the spirit leaving the body. Let the surviving animal know the details about what has happened to his friend. We advise you to talk to your surviving pet just as you would to anyone else who has lost someone he loves — with sympathy and by recalling the happy moments. If nothing else, these conversations will help you to feel better.

CHILDREN AND PET LOSS

Pets are family members. Children relate to animals as their friends, protectors, and playmates. When the family pet dies, it is often the child's first exposure to death and can cause him or her to feel confused and upset.

Jo Ellen Carson wrote about a little cat who became an integral part of her family. When the cat died accidentally, their home felt empty without him. Jo Ellen wrote:

When we first picked our silky gray kitten out of the litter (or rather when he picked us), we knew he was special — just what our family needed. His name came to my daughter Kyra in a dream, but we didn't trust it at first. (Caspar seemed more like a name for a ghost!) But after trying on other names, we ran across Kasper on the Internet and learned that it is a Persian name meaning treasured secret. The perfect name after all.

Kasper befriended each member of our family, singling out each one in his own unique way. He kept thirteen-year-old Kyra company while she did her homework, then cuddled with seven-year-old Brynn as she drifted off to sleep. After my husband, Todd, and I went to bed, Kasper would stretch out across one of our necks, purring loudly.

Kasper was truly a "treasured secret," giving love — and drawing out our family's love with each day that passed. We couldn't wait to get home from school or work to see him. He seemed to know just what we needed, whether it was comfort or playful distraction. His favorite morning ritual was to hop in the wet shower and watch in fascination as the water droplets ran down the walls.

On the day that Kasper accidentally got out of the house, he had been especially affectionate. But it seemed as if he had just disappeared. We still had not found him by bedtime, so I opened a window, thinking I would hear his meow sometime in the night.

Early the next morning, after my husband left for work, he walked back into the house and broke the news that he had found Kasper. The cat had been hit by a car on our quiet dead-end street.

It was hard to believe that Kasper was gone. We missed him terribly, and the house felt empty without him. But as I reflected on our "treasured secret," I recognized what this little spiritual teacher had given us. Kasper knew no fear. He stepped forward into the adventure of life without looking back. He epitomized unconditional love. His gifts, in turn, have helped each of us in my family to grow beyond fear and into greater love.

Entire books are devoted to helping children with pet loss, providing substantial practical suggestions. We've included the books that we currently recommend in the Resources section of this book. One of the best books we've found for guiding adults and therapists through the complex issues surrounding a child's first experience with death, pet accidents, missing pets, and pets who are placed out for adoption is *Pet Loss and Children*, by Cheri Barton Ross. It has a foreword by Deborah Antinori, the author of another resource we highly recommend, *Journey through Pet Loss*, also described in the Resources section.

For children, you can hardly do better than Fred Rogers's book *When a Pet Dies*. In the introduction Rogers writes, "As you and your children look at the photos and read the text, I hope you'll find it possible to share your real feelings about a pet's dying. As for what happens after death, I believe that's best discussed in light of each family's traditions and beliefs. Those traditions and beliefs are important things to share with your children if and when they ask!"[7]

From our research on children and pet loss, as well as our experiences with our own children, we have compiled a list of the major considerations for helping youngsters deal with their grief.

AVOID EUPHEMISMS. When telling children what happened, avoid euphemisms such as, "We had to put Buffy to sleep," "Buffy got sick and died," "God took Buffy to heaven," or "Buffy has gone away." All of these ways of describing death can be confusing to children and can cause them to fear going to sleep or getting sick, to fear or feel angry toward God, or to believe the pet will come back someday. Linda M. Peterson writes in *Surviving the Heartbreak of Choosing Death for Your Pet* that a healthy, clear, factual explanation to a child might sound something like this: "When Max died, his body stopped working. He [couldn't] breathe, eat, hear, see, go to the bathroom, or play with his friends anymore." She suggests that a child will be encouraged to talk about feelings concerning death and loss if told something like "Max has died and will never be alive again. We will miss Max. Right now we are feeling very sad. It will take time, but after a while, we will remember Max without feeling quite so sad. We will always love Max and remember how wonderful he was and all the fun we had with him."[8]

Involve your children in the animal's memorial service and rituals or in creating mementos to commemorate your pet's life. Tell your child what has been done with the animal's body.

EXPLAIN DEATH AGE-APPROPRIATELY. Remember that children grieve differently from adults. Their sadness will come and go and may recur over longer periods of time. Children also deal with grief according to their level of maturation. They will be able to understand death only in ways that are appropriate for their age. Explaining death has similarities to teaching children about sex: it's best to let the children ask questions and to answer them with only as much information as they require at the time.

USE ART AND STORYTELLING. Often children cannot express or articulate what they are feeling with regard to grief, loss, and death. Sit with them while they draw pictures of their animal friend and talk about him, telling their own stories of what it was like to live with the pet and how they feel now that the pet is gone. Encourage children to play and act out what they think has happened to the animal and what they believe is going on with the animal physically and spiritually.

DON'T MAKE DEATH SOUND TOO HAPPY. Explain what happens after death according to your own philosophical, cultural, religious, or spiritual beliefs without making the child think that death is such a "happy" event that it is preferable to living.

GRIEVE WITH YOUR CHILDREN. Don't be afraid to grieve in front of your child. When you mourn openly, you let your child know that it's okay to be sad, to cry, and to miss the family pet.

USE STORYTELLING AND ART TO ALLEVIATE REGRETS. Through storytelling, play, or art, discern if your child feels responsible for the animal's death. Children may believe that somehow they caused the death, perhaps by not taking care of or feeding the animal properly. You can gently correct these assumptions.

GET PROFESSIONAL HELP, IF NECESSARY. If your child is grieving excessively, withdrawing, or acting out, don't hesitate to get professional help. A counselor who specializes in children's grieving can do wonders to help a child sort through his or her thoughts and emotions about a pet's death. A child therapist can also help the entire family deal with other issues that may be complicating their grief over the loss of a pet.

ALLOW THE GRIEF PROCESS TO TAKE ITS NATURAL COURSE BY NOT RUSHING INTO A NEW ADOPTION. Wait a while before adopting another pet. Let your child have all the time he or she needs for mourning. If or when your child wants a new pet, explain the ways in which this new one may be different from your previous pet.

Perhaps Wallace Sife best sums up the advice for grieving children and their caregivers when he writes, "Reminisce, fondly, with the children about the pet. Use pictures, if possible. Associate positive, good events with the pet's memory. Emphasize that as long as we remember and love that pet, he or she will always be part of us."[9]

As you emerge from the initial phases of shock and disbelief, you are likely to begin seeking ways to pull your life and your emotions back together. This is when you start taking the risk of walking across bridges that, even if unsteadily at first, eventually reconnect you with life.

MEDITATION

Who Are Your Covered Bridges?

Reflect on who your covered bridges might be. Who are the people, services, and organizations that can support and shelter you through your grieving and healing process?

MEDITATION

Who Else Is Hurting?

The other pets in my home are grieving over your absence. These are the things I will do to help them with their bereavement:_____.

Family members in my home are grieving over your loss. I will help my family to cope with your death by:_____.

In the Appendix the meditation "The Rest of Our Animal Family" will help you contemplate on additional steps to take for helping other pets in the family grieve and heal.

CHAPTER FIVE

Swinging Bridges
Rituals That Heal and Beliefs That Cause Pain

Have you ever been at sea in a dense fog, when it seemed as if a tangible white darkness shut you in, and the great ship, tense and anxious, groped her way toward the shore with plummet and sounding-line, and you waited with beating heart for something to happen? I was like that ship before my education began, only I was without compass or sounding-line, and had no way of knowing how near the harbour was. "Light! Give me light!" was the wordless cry of my soul, and the light of love shone on me in that very hour.

— Helen Keller, *The Story of My Life*

After the loss of an animal companion, you are probably feeling wobbly and unsafe, longing for the light of love that once shone through the eyes of your pet. You are in the midst of a transition from being blessed with the steadfastness of an animal's love to tossing about on a roiling, uncertain sea. You may be yearning for the stability of being greeted by one who always cared, and wondering how to make it through another day without the constancy of animal companionship.

This is when you need a swinging bridge.

A swinging bridge is not meant to support you for a long time. Swinging bridges, made of rope or roughly hewn planks, or perhaps suspended by cables, feel unstable when you first step onto them. Yet they get the job done. They take you across your rivers of grief. They offer temporary yet practical solutions for your journey until you no longer need them or can replace them with permanent structures.

In this chapter, you have the opportunity to move across swinging bridges to honor an animal who had a profound impact on your life.

RECOGNIZING WHAT IS MISSING NOW

In "Dear Dogs," an essay that Lincoln Newton Kinnicutt wrote in 1915, Kinnicutt defines what most of us have found in our animal companions: "You know us in many ways as no human being knows us, for every hour of your life you wish to be near, and often you are our most intimate companion and the best friend we have in the world."[1]

Your animal companion becomes your mirror. She reflects your authentic and, often, your hidden self. With her qualities of unselfishness and acceptance, she shows you what you can become if your heart is as true as hers. Some say that animal lovers project their needs and desires onto their pets. To some extent, the accusation is true. Who hasn't looked into the eyes of uncritical animals and wanted to be more like what we perceive them to be? Shirley MacLaine writes about her dog, "Terry returns my love so openly, so fiercely, that I begin to see what is possible between human beings."[2]

Now that your animal companion is gone, you not only may have lost a good friend, you also might be bereft of an exercise buddy, a "child" who made you feel needed, a protector of your home, a terrific listener, an entertaining comic, or all of the above.

The veterinarian Martin Goldstein, in his wonderful book *The Nature of Animal Healing*, remarks on the way people and pets relate to one another at every level of their spiritual interdependence. He says, "I think that a pet and his owner both have spirits, that those spirits interact, and that the interaction affects the mental and physical well-being of both."[3]

TRY THIS EXERCISE

Make a list of the needs your animal companion filled. Next to each kind of interaction, jot ideas you have for how you could temporarily meet those needs without her. For example, if your pet always slept next to you in bed, consider getting a soft, furry plush toy so that you can feel a comforting weight nearby at night. Think about the people, organizations, other animals, or creative ways that could help you to fill the holes in your life left by the loss.

Ideas for Meeting the Needs My Pet Fulfilled

Physical Needs: _____

Emotional Needs: _____

Mental or Psychological Needs: _____

Spiritual Needs: _____

Observe if or when the temporary solutions you have chosen should become permanent. Make adjustments to your list. For example, you may decide to walk a different route than the one you used to take with your dog. Then you may find the features of the new route enjoyable and want to continue using it.

It is a good idea to return to this list to see if your needs are changing or diminishing. You may not realize right away that your spiritual needs, for example, have been met in surprising ways. Mary Glasgo wrote to us about her cat Jessica, a fourteen-year-old tabby who had never been sick. Mary was shocked when the vet diagnosed a malignant cancer in Jessica's lymphatic system. On the morning that Jessica died, Mary was inundated with work responsibilities. She lived quite a distance from the vet's office, so she wasn't able to make it there in time to say goodbye to her cat. Mary called the vet and asked, "Will you please tell Jessica how much I love her?" When Mary hung up the telephone, she bowed her head and released Jessica to God, praying that the cat would not have to continue suffering. As soon as she made this true act of surrender, the vet called to say that Jessica had passed away, purring to the very end.

Several years later, Mary's husband, Lee, who had been paralyzed and bedridden with cancer for some time, was near death. As Mary and her daughter sat by his bedside, Mary thought about how Jessica had left this world at the moment when Mary had sincerely stopped holding on to her. So she assured her husband that after his death, she would be fine, that God would watch over her and the rest of the family. She wrote, "Lee passed away peacefully, knowing that I [had] released him and would be all right. Later, I felt grateful for my dear little Jessica, who had died at the moment of my greatest surrender and taught me how to trust and let go."

The Appendix contains three additional meditations that enable you to reflect on how to fill the deep hole left by the pet you have lost. They are "The Golden Thread of Love," "My Needs Now That You Are Gone," and "You Made Me Laugh."

LETTING GO OF ANGER

Lingering in the wake of surrender may be anger — a muddiness of mind that keeps you mired in grief and loss. Letting go of anger can become the swinging bridge that takes you to the other side, away from a pile of pain.

For some people, pet loss creates a spiritual turning point in their lives. It sometimes brings a person closer to his or her house of worship, its leaders, and its congregation. For others, pet loss arouses anger at religious or spiritual systems and at God.

When you try to talk about animals and the afterlife, you may find that members of your congregation, or the people who lead it, are out of tune with the belief that you will meet your pet in the afterlife. At this point, you may feel torn between what you believe, or may have experienced spiritually, and the orthodox teachings of your religion. The death of such a precious and important creature as your pet might cause you to question your beliefs, faith, and theology.

If a spiritual director or counselor says that only humans have souls and that you will not ever see your animal friend again, you may be tempted to walk or run away and never return. The poet Pat O'Cotter expresses these feelings well in a verse from "A Malamute Dog": "You can't tell me God would have Heaven / So a man couldn't mix with his friends — / That we are doomed to meet disappointment / When we come to the place the trail ends."[4]

Members of your congregation and its spiritual leaders may be sympathetic to your pain without believing that God will let you be with your pet again. They may think that your questions about the afterlife are merely symptomatic of intense grief and that when you feel better, you'll realize that being reunited with your pet is not possible.

Hindu and Buddhist teachings support the idea that animals are sentient beings who go to heaven and reincarnate. Some religious traditions are amenable to holding a memorial service for an animal companion. Others might see such an activity as unnecessary or even sacrilegious. Carrie wrote to us in a letter about the death of her beloved dog, Francesco, "My religion teaches that animals don't go to heaven, but I know that they do. If there really is a heaven, I know Francesco is there."[5]

Religions run the gamut of beliefs. The Reverend Mary Piper, an Episcopal priest and hospital chaplain, wrote an inspiring story about a "moose messenger" for our book *God's Messengers: What Animals Teach Us about the Divine*. After her dog Eunice died, she asked for a sign that Eunice was with God. Moments after she and her husband separately requested that the most unlikely appearance of a moose be that sign, a moose walked by, in full daylight, right through their backyard, in answer to their prayer. The Reverend Piper used this experience with the moose as the basis for the Sunday's sermon at her church.[6]

In *The Loss of a Pet* by Wallace Sife, Rabbi Balfour Brickner, the senior rabbi emeritus of the Stephen Wise Free Synagogue in New York City, is quoted about the Jewish beliefs on mourning and pet loss: "Out of this tradition [the compassionate consideration for the welfare of animals, codified in Jewish law], it is legitimate to extract an attitude of sympathetic response to the loss of a pet and to the tender administration of a pet's remains. A pet, having brought joy to the life of its owner, is as deserving of loving care in death as it was in its lifetime. However, after its death and disposal, one is not expected to mourn excessively or become involved in bizarre or unnecessarily expensive practices, any more than such expression would be tolerated after the death of a person. Death is a part of life, and after death and reasonable mourning, life is to continue normally as quickly as possible."[7]

HOW TO HANDLE A DISAGREEMENT WITH YOUR RELIGION'S BELIEFS

So the moral of the story is, you decide what you believe. Our advice is to adhere to the old adage about not throwing out the baby with the bathwater. Until you are certain that you and your religion are completely at odds on most issues, we advise you not to abandon it. We have seen people turn away from religions that heretofore had provided both community and comfort, thus making themselves feel even more alone, vulnerable, and angry at God.

Perhaps, with patience, you can find a way to reconcile what you believe about animals, souls, and the afterlife with the teachings of your religion by agreeing to disagree on this one point. But perhaps the disagreement you have with your religion heralds the beginning of the end of your relationship with that tradition. If so, you will have to deal with that split. Following are some suggestions that provide swinging bridges to help you past the difficulties of disagreeing with your religion.

- Accept that there is a disconnect between what you believe and what your religion teaches about humanity's relationship with animals and about the spiritual nature of animals. Continue to find comfort in the teachings, members, and leaders of your religion that harmonize with you.
- Consider finding a different congregation or spiritual guide whose beliefs are in closer alignment with yours. In most religions, you will find that congregations and leaders have differing ways of interpreting the fundamental and ancillary beliefs of that religion.
- Express your anger at God verbally (screaming or shouting, if you have to) and by writing a letter to the Divine. Anger at God is a natural part of grieving when life seems unfair. Allow yourself to express your rage out loud or on paper until it becomes less intense. Be assured that God can handle your anger and keep loving you.
- Let God be God. Regardless of what anyone tells you concerning animals in heaven or the afterlife, know that God can do anything. If animals are necessary for your heavenly happiness and reward, God is certainly capable of having them in heaven with you. No earthly laws or theologies can dictate to the Divine.
- Read books and talk to people who will reassure you and make you feel better about your loss and God's role in it. In the Resources section we have listed some helpful books that explain what various religions teach about animals, souls, and heaven.

- Trust your own experiences and inner spiritual guidance. You may have experiences that are clearly indicative of the animal's continuing spiritual presence and love. Unless you allow it, no one can take these experiences away from you or diminish them.

MEDITATION

How can you build swinging bridges that will take you from shaken religious beliefs to a sense of peace, comfort, and stability?

RITUALS TO HELP YOU MOURN

Rituals provide you with ways to simultaneously honor and release your pet and the way of life that you miss sharing with him.

Pets require you to have routines. Consider changing those everyday habits, at least slightly, so that you are not faced with a reminder of your loss of companionship while your emotions are still raw. In other words, give yourself a break. If you always got up early to feed the dog, sleep later or at least awaken at a different time. On the other hand, if there are routines that comfort you, go ahead and keep following them. Perhaps your cat slept on a certain blanket, and it still has his smell. Sniffing this blanket from time to time may bring back pleasant memories of that special scent you associate with the cat curling up to sleep with you. Keep doing what feels better. Stop whatever makes you feel worse. Taking care of yourself can be as simple as that.

Following are rituals others have found helpful at various stages of the grieving and healing process. Always check in with yourself as you try to follow them. See which one is in harmony with how you're feeling today.

TRY THIS EXERCISE

Select rituals that help you to remember and honor your animal companion in ways that console, uplift, and inspire you.

- Speak out loud (when no one else is around) or think thoughts to the spirit of your pet. Express how much you miss him and recall the things that you loved the most about your life together. Call his name when you return home or leave the house and when you go to bed or wake up in the morning. Don't forget to listen to whatever thoughts, feelings, and images may come back to you during these times of spiritual communication. "Our Song" is a lovely additional meditation in the Appendix that allows you to use the lyrics and melody of a song to release feelings of gratitude for your angel animal.

- Start an album of favorite photos of your pet. Write captions that express your feelings and capture the memories that the pictures bring to mind. Add your children's drawings and remembrances. Talk with trusted family members and friends as you show them photos and mementos of your pet.

- Wear a special piece of jewelry, a scarf, or your pet's identification tag. Put something in your pocket that reminds you of your animal companion. When you look at it or touch it, remember the happy times.

- Make a memorial box with your pet's favorite toy, a leash, collar, lock of hair or feather, whisker, paw print (if you have one), food dish, laminated photo, and any other items that remind you of your animal companion. Place the memorial box and the urn with the animal's ashes in a safe spot where you won't have to see them all the time.

- Write a letter to or make an audio recording with memories of your animal companion. Pour out your emotions and thoughts. Keep writing or recording until you start remembering happy times, funny things your pet did, and peaceful feelings. Invite others who knew your pet to write and record their thoughts and memories, too.

- Write a eulogy or a prayer to use in a memorial service. The playwright Eugene O'Neill wrote "The Last Will and Testament of Silverdene Emblem O'Neill" to console his wife, Carlotta, after the death of Blemie, the family's Dalmatian. He wrote it as if it came from the dog, ending it with the words, "No matter how deep my sleep I shall hear you, and not all the power of death can keep my spirit from wagging a grateful tail."[8] You can also share eulogies and prayers with others on websites that publish them. See the Resources section for some of these sites.

- Make a journal of your memories, feelings, and dreams. See if you are getting more assistance with healing than you realized.
- Write a poem or story. Compose a song. Create a piece of artwork that will always remind you and others of your animal companion's life and personality.
- Walk along a trail that you and your animal companion used to take together. Pick up stones and twigs along the way. When you return home, arrange them in a beautiful dish.
- Light a candle at a certain time each day. While the flame flickers, remember your animal friend fondly and ask for her spiritual presence and help.
- Commemorate your pet's everlasting place in your heart during the holidays with a stocking that has his name on it. Do something meaningful to honor his birthday or the anniversary of when you first met.

Be sure to include your children in rituals that are appropriate for their age. The use of rituals, tributes, and memorial services can bring your family closer and become a lasting and loving memory for you and your children.

LASTING TRIBUTES TO YOUR ANIMAL COMPANION

Whereas rituals are everyday things you can do to commemorate an animal who blessed you with his love and presence, tributes are more formal ways of demonstrating that your pet left an indelible imprint on your life and the lives of others. In *Pet Loss: A Spiritual Guide*, Julia Harris writes, "In addition to the time, effort, and expense of making final arrangements for your pet, you have an inner demand to make your pet's memory live on in a positive manner."[9]

- Order a plaque or a gravestone marker to put near your pet's grave or in a place of honor.
- Dedicate a park bench to your animal. Choose a park where you love to walk and will see it often.
- Hire an artist to paint a portrait or create a sculpture of your pet's likeness. Have a musician write and record a song about your pet. Place these mementos in a prominent spot in your home where, eventually, they will always bring a smile to your face.
- Make a donation in your pet's honor to an animal shelter, rescue group, animal welfare organization, or charity. This will help you feel better and also could save the life of another animal or human.
- Plant a tree, a garden, or flowers to commemorate your animal companion. This kind of tribute beautifies the environment just as your pet brought beauty to your life.
- Place an ad in the newspaper to publish your pet's obituary. One couple did this in their local paper, and their tribute gave the newspaper the idea to make pet obituaries a regular feature.

The next chapter offers three types of memorial services. You can use them to gather together with those who want to join in your bereavement as you remember and honor your animal companion.

MEDITATION

Commemorate Your Pet

What do you want to do to publicly commemorate that a brave and wonderful spirit once lived and now is gone?

MEDITATION

The Shimmering Light of My Dreams

Come to me in my dreams. I long to see how you glow without your physical body.

I am asking for dreams about things we used to do together. I will write down my dreams in a journal and reread them from time to time. I will make the connection between my dreams and the love that you are still trying to give to me.

I close my eyes and replay a dream of you in my mind. Can I catch a glimpse of you and where you are now?

CHAPTER SIX

Memorial Bridges
Memorial Services for Angel Animals

Love all of God's creation, both the whole of it and every grain of sand. Love every leaf, every ray of God's light. Love animals, love plants, love each thing. If you love each thing, you will perceive the mystery of God in things. Once you have perceived it, you will begin tirelessly to perceive more and more of it every day. And you will come at last to love the whole world with an entire, universal love.

— Fyodor Dostoevsky, *The Brothers Karamazov*

Memorial bridges are named after significant events or larger-than-life figures in history. With their presence they ensure that their namesakes will never be forgotten. So it is with the memorials that we create in honor of the remarkable creatures who have forever changed our lives for the better.

The memorial services in this chapter are designed to be used whole or in part. You can mix and match pieces of the services, rearrange the order, make additions, or eliminate whatever you want.

If you would like a secular service that commemorates your pet but doesn't mention God, the soul, or heaven, or that is otherwise nonreligious, use the "I Remember You" memorial service.

The "All God's Creatures" memorial service should be appropriate for people in any denomination of the Christian faith or practitioners of Judaism.

The "Together Again" memorial service refers to God, the soul, heaven, and a belief in reincarnation. It would be most appropriate for people who are of the Jewish or Hindu faiths, who practice Buddhism, or who consider themselves to be nonspecific or eclectic in their spiritual beliefs.

Choose whichever service most appeals to you and consoles you. As an optional feature for any of the services, you can close the ceremony with a reading of the Rainbow Bridge story from the Introduction to this book.

In planning the memorial service, pay close attention to your dreams, your intuition, and any communication that may be coming from the spiritual essence of the animal you are honoring.

We received a story from Vineeta Anand, a woman whose adorable little rabbit, Shunya, appeared in her friend Katharine's dream shortly after the animal's death. Shunya's name means "zero" in Sanskrit, which is symbolic of the circle of life and death. Even after death, this little rabbit lived up to his name by teaching his human companions much about the ongoing presence of loved ones.

Vineeta had intended to scatter Shunya's ashes in the sacred Ganges River in India when she visited there in the summer. But Shunya had other preferences. In Katharine's dream, Shunya revealed that he hadn't wanted to leave Vineeta and he didn't want to be near the water. Vineeta didn't immediately understand what the dream meant. When she didn't change her plans, Shunya started making noisy, invisible appearances in Vineeta's home. Vineeta heard the sounds of a closet door slamming, paper crumpling, footsteps racing up the stairs, and an animal's nails scratching on the wooden floor. She finally decided to call in paranormal investigators, who confirmed the unusual supernatural activity with an infrared motion detector. Finally Vineeta remembered Katharine's dream and interpreted it correctly. Vineeta wrote, "Like a typical rabbit, Shunya was afraid of the water. He did not want his ashes scattered in a river."

So instead of taking Shunya's ashes to the Ganges, Vineeta held a memorial service for him with a few friends in a beautiful park on a snowy Saturday afternoon. They spread rabbit food in a circle and chanted prayers together. Vineeta wrote, "We saw three herds of deer that day, and the birds chirped in the woods. These were good omens, and I knew Shunya would be happy."[1]

KEEP IT SIMPLE

As you plan your pet's memorial service, keep the ceremony simple and short. Hold the service in a place that is meaningful to you and was to your pet. This could be at home, in a park where you walked together, by water where you frolicked, or at the pet cemetery where your pet is buried. Invite friends who knew your animal companion. Ask everyone to turn off cell phones and beepers. If the ceremony is in a home, unplug the phone and turn off the answering machine. You may want to tape-record the service; if you do, ask participants to speak directly into the tape recorder's microphone.

If you wish, create a sacred space by having a table in the center of the group of mourners who have gathered. Cover the table with a white cloth and arrange lighted candles, flowers, and framed photos of your pet. Set aside some extra candles, one for each mourner.

You might wish to play some sacred or uplifting music at the memorial service. If so, bring the equipment you will need or ask someone to play or sing the songs you have selected.

Prior to the service, ask participants to plan to share something that they miss about your deceased pet or to recall a special time they spent with him. At the ceremony, give each person a candle. When the person speaks, she can light her candle as a symbol of the light of love in her heart and then share her memory of the animal. Afterward, she can blow out the candle as a symbol of the light that has left this world. Then she can take one of the flowers from the table to signify that the animal's beauty and love remain with her.

If you are scattering your pet's ashes at the service, position yourself where the wind won't blow them back onto you or your guests.

Most of all, know that whether you or someone you've asked leads the service, you can't and won't make any mistakes. Your love and sincerity will shine through each step along the way.

Materials you will need:

- Candles, for the table and one for each participant
- Matches
- Framed photo of your pet
- Flowers, enough for each participant

- Urn or box with your pet's ashes
- This book
- The Rainbow Bridge story (optional)
- Music (optional)
- Tape recorder, video recorder, or other recording equipment (optional)

I REMEMBER YOU MEMORIAL SERVICE

Thank you for coming together to honor the life and memory of _____ [pet's name].

_____ [pet's name], you became the seasons of my life. You entered it with the graciousness of spring. On _____ [date of death], you left with the finality of autumn. Like a perpetual summer, your innocence warmed each of my days. As silently as falling snow on a winter night, you quietly listened to my secret sorrows.

_____ [pet's name], you became the forces of Nature in my life. You made me smile, even as day-to-day disappointments rained and storms swirled my anxious thoughts. With your playfulness, you coaxed me to enjoy the stillness inside each moment. No star glistened brighter in the night sky. No wave lapped more steadily against the shore. No sunbeam more happily heralded the dawn.

Then Death tolled its mighty bell and called you away. My tears would not stop. My emptiness would not be filled. My loneliness would not end.

Now I want to express gratitude for the gift of your generous companionship. You reminded me of all the good that it is possible to find in this world — loyalty, selflessness, courage, devotion, and unconditional love. Memories of what you taught me will keep you in my heart forever.

Today, we celebrate the Circle of Life that returns you

to nourish Earth, sweeten Wind, strengthen Fire, and enrich Water.

Now, I invite each of you to share a fond memory of _____ [*pet's name*] or of what you will miss most about [*him/her*]. Please light your candle as a symbol of the love that _____ [*pet's name*] brought to our lives. After you have spoken, blow out your candle to symbolize the light that has left this world. Then take a flower to signify the love and beauty _____ [*pet's name*] gave to us, which will never die.

Each person lights a candle, shares a happy memory of your pet, and takes a flower from the table. You can begin or end this sharing with your own memory. After everyone who wants to speak has spoken, thank the group.

Play or have someone perform music, if you have planned for it during the ceremony.

If you are scattering your pet's ashes, do so now.

Close the service with the following poem:

This is a poem of the Teton Sioux called "I Sing for the Animals":

"Out of the earth
I sing for them,
A Horse nation
I sing for them.
Out of the earth
I sing for them,
The animals,
I sing for them."[2]

End of ceremony.

ALL GOD'S CREATURES MEMORIAL SERVICE

Thank you for coming together to honor the life and memory of _____ [pet's name].

This is a reading from Job 12:7–10:

"But ask now the beasts, and they shall teach thee; and the fowls of the air, and they shall tell thee. Or speak to the earth, and it shall teach thee: and the fishes of the sea shall declare unto thee. Who knoweth not in all these that the hand of the Lord hath wrought this? In Whose hand is the soul of every living thing, and the breath of all mankind."[3]

_____ [pet's name], you have returned to God, the Creator of earth and sky, humans and animals, and I will miss you. But I know that heaven would not be heaven without you there. So I believe that God will reunite us in body and spirit. We will be welcomed with your divine embrace. _____ [pet's name], you are waiting for me at the Rainbow Bridge, and I thank you. We will cross the bridge together to share an eternity of infinite bliss.

[Or:]

_____ [pet's name], God gave me the gifts of your presence, your loyalty, and your courage, and I am grateful. With your faithfulness and compassion, you reminded me how God loves — unconditionally. I miss you, my friend, but I know that God comforts us through our deepest sorrows. As He does with me, God comforts all of His creatures. He watched over and cared for you in life. When you walked through the Valley of the Shadow of Death, you feared no evil, for He is always with you.

Or begin the service by reciting a favorite prayer or singing a hymn.

Now, I invite each of you to share a fond memory of _____ [pet's name] or of what you will miss most about [him/her]. Please light your candle as a symbol of the love that _____ [pet's name] brought to our lives. After you have spoken, blow out your candle to symbolize the light that has left this world. Then take a flower to signify the love and beauty _____ [pet's name] gave to us, which will never die.

Each person lights a candle, shares a happy memory of your pet, and takes a flower from the table. You can begin or end this sharing with your own memory. After everyone who wants to speak has spoken, thank the group.

Play or have someone perform music, if you have planned for it during the ceremony.

If you are scattering your pet's ashes, do so now.

Close the service with the following scriptural passage:

This is a reading from Genesis 9:12–17:

"God said to Noah and his sons, 'As a sign of this everlasting covenant, which I am making with you and with all living beings, I am putting my bow in the clouds. It will be the sign of my covenant with the world. Whenever I cover the sky with clouds and the rainbow appears, I will remember my promise to you and to all animals that a flood will never again destroy all living beings. When the rainbow appears in the clouds, I will see it and remember the everlasting covenant between me and all living beings on earth. That is the sign of the promise which I am making to all living beings.'"[4] *End of ceremony.*

TOGETHER AGAIN MEMORIAL SERVICE

Thank you for coming together to honor the life and memory of _____ [*pet's name*].

This is an excerpt from a poem, "To Roxy," written by Grace Strong Dignowity around 1935. It expresses the loss I feel for _____ [*pet's name*].

"Loyal, loving, faithful, brave
Until my saddest day
When you went alone your lonely road
But here I had to stay.
Oh you will live on in my heart
My little friend so true,
And memories of you fill my mind
Until I go to you".[5]

_____ [*pet's name*], you have reminded me that we are all connected by a golden thread of love, which weaves invisibly through life's fabric. When I felt pain, you ministered to me. When I laughed, you joined in my joy. Our hearts beat in unison to the rhythm of our spiritual partnership, for you taught me how to love.

Come to me in my dreams, dear one. Offer comfort by letting me see the shining brightness of you, glowing without the physical body that once clothed your spiritual greatness.

Know that I release you into the shimmering Light. I drift with you into the blissful Sound. I unite with you in the embrace of Divine Love. As in life, you continue to be my wise teacher, my compassionate friend, and my intuitive guide. You show me how to live in the stillness of now.

Rest, my dear companion. Saint Francis, patron saint of animals, will help us to heal and to nourish ourselves during your transition from life to death.

[Or:]

From reading the Tanach, Ecclesiastes 3:19–21, I know that both humans and animals have God's help during the transition from life to death. It is written: "For that which befalleth the sons of men befalleth beasts; even one thing befalleth them; as the one dieth, so dieth the other; yea, they have all one breath; so that man hath no preeminence above a beast; for all is vanity. All go unto one place; all are of the dust, and all return to dust. Who knoweth the spirit of man whether it goeth upward, and the spirit of the beast whether it goeth downward to the earth?"[6]

[Or:]

If you find that, as a soul and a sentient being, you want to return to be with me in a new body at another time, always know that you have a place in my heart. All I ask is that you let me know you are here and where I can find you. I will joyfully bring you back home, and we will share yet one more life together.

When my time comes to go to the Rainbow Bridge, I will see you there. We will walk across it together and never be parted again. For as long as our love remains strong, nothing can break our spiritual bond.

Now, I invite each of you to share a fond memory of

_____ [*pet's name*] or of what you will miss most about [*him/her*]. Please light your candle as a symbol of the love that _____ [*pet's name*] brought to our lives. After you have spoken, blow out your candle to symbolize the light that has left this world. Then take a flower to signify the love and beauty _____ [*pet's name*] gave to us, which will never die.

Each person lights a candle, shares a happy memory of your pet, and takes a flower from the table. You can begin or end this sharing with your own memory. After everyone who wants to speak has spoken, thank the group.

Play or have someone perform music, if you have planned for it during the ceremony. If you are scattering your pet's ashes, do so now.

With love, chant or sing together a holy name for God, such as God, HU (pronounced like the word hue*), Jesus, Yahweh, Lord, Allah, Mother Goddess, Sacred, or Divine. Or chant a mantra, such as* om, *to uplift the spirit and bring enlightenment to the moment.*

Close the service with the following psalm:
This is a reading from Psalm 65:12–13:
"The pastures are filled with flocks;
        the hillsides are full of joy.
The fields are covered with sheep;
        the valleys are full of wheat.
Everything shouts and sings for joy."[7]
End of ceremony.

INCLUDE THE OTHER ANIMALS

We'd like to close this chapter with a story that illustrates how animals appreciate participating in a memorial service. We mentioned earlier that when our beautiful bird Sparkle died, her mate Sunshine needed to spend time grieving over her. So we waited until after he had left her body on the floor of the cage and returned to his perch. He turned his head away in sadness, as if to give his permission for us to remove the body.

Before we took Sparkle out to bury her, we called the other animals in our household and asked each of them if they wanted to say goodbye. We held Sparkle in our hands as first the dog, Taylor, and then the two cats, Cuddles and Speedy, sniffed the bird. As our tears fell, the animals, who had shared their home with Sparkle, silently formed a circle around us. Their grief was palpable. Taylor lowered her head. The cats stretched out on the floor with paws pointing toward Sparkle. For minutes, no one moved. Sunshine watched from his perch.

To join with the animals in the spiritual grace of this farewell, we began to sing HU, a sacred love song to God. As the sound of this lovely chant filled the room, each animal, in turn, stood up and slowly walked away. Sunshine again turned his head away. We knew then that the time had come to bury Sparkle.

We invite you to join us for the last chapter of this book. In it, you will find the help you need, from the universe and from your spiritually tuned-in pet, to reconnect with the happiness and joy of life.

MEDITATION

Meeting You at the Rainbow Bridge

I will see you at the Rainbow Bridge. We will walk across it together and never be parted again. For as long as our love remains strong, nothing can break our spiritual bond.

What does the Rainbow Bridge look like? I am visualizing it now.

Are there other animal companions I have known and loved who are waiting to meet me there?

As we walk across the Rainbow Bridge together, what do we see on the horizon?

MEDITATION

Your Memorial Service

The memorial I had in your honor was special. I had thoughts, feelings, and impressions during the service. I will write them in my journal.

People spoke to me about you. I will write some of the things they said.

While I planned your memorial service, I had dreams, intuitions, and other types of communication that helped me to know what you wanted me to say and do. I will write about some ways you helped me from the Rainbow Bridge to plan your service.

CHAPTER SEVEN

Golden Bridges
Angel Animals and the Afterlife

Whether a wounded hand or a wounded heart, the healing comes from within. In the process, time passes, priorities shift, and life proceeds. However, life is different, for we have changed.

— Janis Amatuzio, *Forever Ours*

The first time we crossed the Golden Gate Bridge over the San Francisco Bay, the sunset flamed against a darkening sky. Walkway lamps began to glow. Their beams bounced off the vermilion paint and glinting steel, slowly enfolding the bridge in a golden light.

This magnificent vision thrilled us with its symbolism of hope and transformation as the day faded into a luminescent night. Millions of people had traveled this way before us. Millions more would come after us. But we were witnessing a moment in eternity that each of us uniquely interpreted. The people in the surrounding cars crossed the same bridge we did, yet each person was probably noticing different aspects of the bridge at that moment. Some were undoubtedly awed by the colorful sunset. Some observed the onset of night, while others focused on the towers' rising lights.

The spiritual aspects of pet loss are golden bridges that carry travelers to the other side of grief and mourning. Each person who has an animal companion leave his or her life will embark on an individual journey. The lights of healing and reconciliation will become visible through the person's own perspective and in his or her own time.

In this chapter we'll share with you what we have learned from the thousands of people who have shared their sacred experiences with our readers and with us over the years. They tell of afterlife visitations, help from spiritual guides, visionary dreams, and remarkable healings. The golden bridges of pet loss have shown people the purpose and destiny of their lives. They have provided firsthand experiences of rebirth and have given people the courage to love once again. Traveling the golden bridges leads to breathtaking vistas of true enlightenment.

AFTERLIFE VISITATIONS BY ANIMALS

Animal communicator Marta Williams writes, "I believe that animals stay close to us in spirit long after they've left their bodies. I think they do this to help us get through the experience."[1] We have received hundreds of letters from people whose animal companions made their presence known in an unmistakable way after death.

Following are many of the most frequently reported ways in which animals remind people that only the physical body leaves at death, and that the spirit and love live on. People report animals who, after death:

- Scratch or knock at the door
- Pad or make the sound of clicking claws along floors
- Press against the person's body with a definite feeling of weight
- Shake the bed as if jumping on or off it
- Purr, meow, bark, or snore audibly enough for more than one person to hear
- Leave paw prints or food around food bowls
- Make a depression in the bed linens where they used to sleep
- Emit a burst of familiar scent in places that were previously free of pet odor
- Drop a favorite toy, which has been put away or lost, in a spot where it will be easily found
- Set off some kind of electrical charge that causes a clock alarm to go off, lights to flicker, or the telephone to ring at the same time that the death or burial occurred
- Appear as a glow of golden light or in a light-body so real that the person tries unsuccessfully to touch it
- Lick or kiss the person's skin or tickle with whiskers
- Seem to appear in spirit as a sign or symbol of life after death, such as a butterfly or rainbow, on a significant day or time

Entire books have been written about people's experiences with after-death visitations from animals. One of the best is *Animals and the Afterlife,* by Kim Sheridan. Sheridan researched and wrote her book over a six-year period and assembled hundreds of highly credible accounts. She writes, "It is my intention that others will be comforted by the overwhelming evidence of life after death for animals . . . [and] the highly substantiated notion that our loved ones never really die, no matter their species, no matter their size."[2]

COMMUNICATING WITH ANIMALS
AFTER THEIR DEATH

Animal communicators often tell people that it is possible to make contact with pets after the animals have passed on. Sonya Fitzpatrick writes, "Generally, the essence of the animal's personality while on earth remains around us so that we are able to contact them after their death. Many times they meet up with or even live with the souls of their human loved ones on the other side. They are always around and glad to be able to communicate their feelings with us."[3]

Marta Williams offers an exercise for talking with a deceased pet and connecting with his spirit. She advises asking questions and listening to and trusting the answers you receive. You might ask what it is like where the animal resides now and whether or not the spirit intends to come back into another body.[4]

Laura Scott, a writer and editor who has studied animal communication, wrote to us about an experience she had while contacting Reverend Jacquie Mace's cat Sam. When Jacquie was agonizing over whether to have the fatally ill cat euthanized, Sam communicated to her via Laura. Sam said, "I will always be with you, Jacquie. We are like a woven web. We can't be separated. I will come back to you. Shadow will be my name. Bless you for the love you gave, the home you gave, the food, and the care. Whatever your decision is fine with me. My love will stay with you forever and always. Time does not exist. We're connected and we'll be together again very soon."

Later, after Sam's death, Laura had the impression that the cat's spirit wanted to give Jacquie another message. Laura quickly wrote down what she heard Sam communicate from the other side:

So much peace is here. I have a new spiritual body and can be anywhere I choose. I'm going to rest for a while. Then I will have work to do here. We can choose from many jobs. Helping other animals across the threshold of transition is the job I will be doing. I was helped across by two other Sams! [Laura's sister and a friend both had cats named Sam who had died previously.]

We can never be separated. I am with you always. We are connected, entwined like a web, strongest at the heart center. Do not cry for me, as I am peaceful, happy, joyful, and free. The way I left you was a decision made by God, guiding you in your decisions and giving us time to say our goodbyes and acknowledge the love and learning we shared.

You have so much love to give. Don't say no to loving another animal. We have so much to share and to teach you. And that animal might just be me, making my way back to you.

Love never ends. Love never dies. Love is forever, infinite, everlasting. The web that connects us can never be broken and can only trap love and kindness in its net.

Thank you for rescuing me all those years ago and for

letting me give you the love you so richly deserve. God is blessing you now.

TRY THIS EXERCISE

Ask God, Spirit, Jesus, one of the heavenly protectors of animals, or your guardian angels to guide and connect you with an animal companion who has died. Fill your heart with love for this animal and visualize her. Ask whatever questions you would like answered at this time. Write down the thoughts, impressions, and images that come into your mind and touch your heart. Keep writing fast to bypass the mental censor. Later, contemplate and reflect upon what you have received. Decide if the communication rings true for you.

SPIRITUAL PLANE ANIMAL ADVOCATES

If direct communication with animals isn't comfortable for you, or if you just can't seem to figure out how to do it, you may want to ask for help from the spiritual guides whose mission is to care for the animal kingdom. We know of two in history who are noted for their outstanding love and compassion for animals: Saint Francis of Assisi and Saint Martin of Porres.

Saint Francis had the ability to talk with and listen to the animals. Birds flocked to him. A wild wolf became tame at his request. His love of animals and nature was legendary, and he has been named by the Catholic Church as the patron saint of animals. Many churches throughout the world have clergy who perform the Blessing of the Animals ceremony on or near October 4, the Feast of Saint Francis.

Saint Martin of Porres lived in the fifteenth century and is said to have given love to humans and animals — even vermin — in equal measure. He established a hospital for cats and dogs at his sister's home, where animals were treated with dignity and compassion.[5]

Another spiritual guardian for animals is Prajapati (pronounced prah-jah-PAH-tee). Prajapati is an ECK Master (ECK means "Holy Spirit"). His mission to care for animals is noted in the ancient teachings of Eckankar, the modern-day Religion of the Light and Sound of God. Many people have had spiritual experiences with Prajapati coming to the aid of an animal in distress.[6]

Buddhists consider animals to be sentient beings. In his book *The Loss of a Pet*, Wallace Sife quotes the Venerable Khyongla Rato Rinpoche of the Tibet Center in New York: "When an animal is dying, it is customary to recite the names of the buddhas and bodhisattvas to the animal. Hearing these names is especially helpful at the time of death. After the animal has died, holy people can be requested to pray for the deceased pet. One can also go to the temple and make offerings and pray for the animal."[7] Legend has it that a Buddha named Ratnashikhin promised that if a person or animal heard his name at the moment of death, this would bring about rebirth into a beautiful heaven. Reciting the mantra "Namu Sugata Ratnashikhin" at death, or chanting it afterward, is said to evoke the power of the ancient Buddha's vow.

MEDITATION

Call upon spiritual saints, masters, and other beings who watch out for animals in this world and on other planes. Simply fill your heart with love, become still, and ask for their assistance. You can also make a request that your spiritual mission in this life include assisting animals. It is a most rewarding purpose to fulfill with creatures who never hesitate to express and feel gratitude.

DREAMS OF ANIMALS WHO HAVE DIED

One of the most prevalent golden bridges that people experience is to dream of an animal who has died. The animal appears in 3-D, living color, and in great detail. Invariably the person says the dream was as real as anything that happens to him or her in daily life.

Prior to a pet's death, people often have dreams to prepare them for the event. Carrie wrote to us about her dog Francesco, whom she named after Saint Francis. Unfortunately, Francesco contracted autoimmune liver disease. One night, when the dog was near death, he slept on Carrie's chest for ten-minute intervals. Carrie wrote, "During one of those short sleeps that I took with Francesco, I dreamed of a large body of water and a shore on either side of it. A very large ship was approaching the shore on the right. In the dream, I wondered what this meant. The knowledge came that the dream images represented Life. The left shore was the earth and all who live on it. The right shore, our final destination, was heaven.

The water was the journey. Our goal, I realized in the dream, was to help those we love to make it safely to the final destination. The ship represented each of us helping our loved ones make the journey."[8] This dream became tremendously helpful to Carrie during the next week, when she had to say a final goodbye to her dear Francesco.

Margaret Neylon, a dream interpreter, wrote to us about a dream she had of her deceased cat, Zaggy. Margaret wrote, "My other cat, Ziggy, sleeps on the bed with me. I woke in the middle of the night with the feeling of a cat jumping lightly onto me. The thing that really woke me was the loud purr. It was loud! When I looked, I saw Zaggy. She was well and so happy. She and her living sister Ziggy were rubbing against each other and purring. I said, 'Zaggy, I thought you were dead!' Zaggy came and rubbed her face against me as though she was smiling and she just purred. I know this was more than a dream. I was so grateful for her visit. Although it still hurts to lose her, I know for certain that Zaggy is still around. And even better, that she is happy and well."[9]

Not only have people had dreams in which the deceased pet's spirit returned to reassure them that they were fine, but animals often appear in the dream with important information. Nory McCluskey wrote to us about a dream she had of her lovely harlequin Great Dane, Kiera. Many years after Kiera's death, Nory saw Kiera in a dream. The dog urged Nory to tell her sister, whom Kiera had adored, to immediately have an exam on her right breast. The next day, Nory called and left Kiera's dream message on her sister's voice mail. A couple of days later, her sister called to say that she had been putting off having a breast exam. But because of

Kiera's dream message, she had had a lump on her right breast biopsied. The lump had been worrying her, and she was relieved to have just found out that the growth was benign. Nory's sister said, "I didn't tell anybody about the biopsy because I didn't want people to panic. Tell Kiera thanks for the nudge!" Nory ended her letter by saying, "Listen to your dreams. So what if the still, small voice used to be a bark!"[10]

TRY THIS EXERCISE

Keep a journal of your dreams. If you have been recording your dreams, read back through the journal to see if you have had any dreams with animal companions who have died. What messages might they have been trying to deliver?

GRIEF GAUGES

The superb stage play *Shadowlands*, by William Nicholson, which has also been made into a movie, is the story of Christian theologian and author C. S. Lewis and the grief this Oxford professor felt over the death of his wife, Joy. Lewis had to come to grips with the age-old conundrum of whether loving someone completely is worth the risk and pain of losing the beloved. In the play, Lewis finally concludes, "I find I can live with the pain, after all. The pain, now, is part of the happiness, then. That's the deal."[11]

That is definitely the deal. And it leads to a question that anyone who grieves poses: How will I ever love that way again?

Loss isn't something you "get over." But at some point, your feelings of sadness will diminish. Thoughts of your animal companion will no longer overwhelm you. When you see an animal who looks like your dear friend, you won't burst into tears. You'll find yourself enjoying simple pleasures and friendships again. Your other pets will bring comfort instead of constant reminders of loss. You may even have pangs of guilt over feeling better. There may be things you can do now that you couldn't when your pet was alive, and you like the new freedom. All of these thoughts and feelings are a natural part of the grieving and healing process.

TRY THIS EXERCISE

Put a photo of your pet on your refrigerator or on top of a dresser or mantel. At the end of the day, count how many times you remember looking at the photo and mourning the loss of your pet. Notice when the number of sad thoughts and feelings declines.

GETTING BACK INTO THE RHYTHMS OF LIFE

If you are depressed and your sadness lingers, find a way to help other people or animals. This can take the form of volunteering at an animal shelter or offering a foster home to animals who need temporary assistance. Giving, as a way out of depression, is expressed beautifully in the children's book *Charlotte's Web*, by E. B. White. The spider, Charlotte, nearing the end of her life, says to her friend Wilbur, the pig, "I wove my webs for you because I liked you. After all, what's a life, anyway? We're born, we live a little while, we die. . . . By helping you, perhaps I was trying to lift up my life a trifle. Heaven knows, anyone's life can stand a little of that."[12]

It's surprising how many people have written to or told us that the loss of their beloved pet has led them to fulfill their life's purpose. The death of Christine Davis's dog, Martha, became the catalyst for Christine to write books that have comforted countless others. After her dog had a second stroke and died in her arms, sorrow overwhelmed Christine. She wrote, "I sobbed tears that seemingly had no end. I screamed out at the universe, and when I was too tired to rant outwardly, I went deep inside and curled up into a little ball. I forgot about looking for my true path; I forgot about my husband. I felt deeply, completely alone. Martha had been the first being to truly love me in this life."

While Christine was driving home one day, she cried and called out loud, telling Martha how much she missed the way the dog used to howl with her whenever she sang. At that moment, Christine had a vision of an angel in the sky holding Martha in her arms. Christine heard the angel say, "But she still sings with you!" Comforted by seeing Martha resting in the angel's arms and looking happy and peaceful, Christine went home and continued to meditate on this experience. She heard the message that she should start writing about Martha and remember this vision.

A year after the vision, Martha appeared in her angelic form to

Christine again. Martha gave Christine the title of the book that she should start writing: *For Every Dog an Angel.* The basic outline came to Christine as if it were being dictated. This encounter ended with Christine being told that grieving people were looking for her story.

Afterward, Christine wrote down everything she had heard during the experience, "knowing it was a gift from the universe, and from Martha." Later, she also illustrated the story, formed a company she named Lighthearted Press, and published the book. The book and its sequel, *For Every Cat an Angel,* have become wonderful vehicles for helping people heal.

Christine wrote, "Martha's spirit flows through every page. I feel her presence whenever I do speaking engagements. The response has been most heartwarming. It has been a privilege to participate in this collaborative effort. And although I have always heard having business partners can be rather tricky, I must say the angels have been quite easy to work with!"[13]

An additional exercise in the Appendix, "Peaceful, at Last," will help you to reflect on what to do with all the love your angel animal has brought into your life by passing it along to others who need it.

HOW DO YOU KNOW WHEN YOU'RE READY TO ADOPT ANOTHER PET?

You can't, nor would you want to, replace one pet with another. Each animal is a unique individual with his own personality, habits, opinions, feelings, and spirit. The next pet will probably be very different from the previous one, even if both are the same breed and look alike. Trying to duplicate the experience of one pet with another can be disappointing and can cause you and your family to have expectations that the new arrival cannot possibly meet. But there comes a time for most of us when having a furry, fuzzy, feathery, or scaly critter in our homes again is the only cure for what ails us.

It is important, though, not to short-circuit the grieving process for yourself, your family, and your other pets. Give yourself whatever time you need to fully mourn, miss, and reconcile yourself to the loss of your animal companion. Still, there are no hard-and-fast rules. Some people adopt another pet right away. Some wait for years. Others never do live with an animal in their homes again but prefer to volunteer at animal shelters or try new adventures. We have received letters from people who decided to adopt a different type of animal the next time around, and the new experience has been satisfying for them.

Often the new adoption takes place after an animal chooses you, appearing on your doorstep one day, tapping you on the shoulder at an animal shelter, jumping into your arms, or popping out of a litter to untie your shoelaces (something that happened to us twice). Nancy Miller wrote about a beautiful long-haired Siamese cat, Siam, who started showing up on her porch around the same time that her blue parakeet, Willow, died. Siam wouldn't come indoors, but the night before Willow passed away, he ventured inside, ate a bit, and went upstairs to sleep on Nancy's porch roof. But he did not stay the night. Nancy says, "The next morning, Siam strolled inside, let me love him a bit, and has been here ever since. Siam's loving presence and his agreement to join my family exactly when he did has made the loss of little Willow much easier for me. And I'm a person who thought I'd never have a cat."[14]

As we always say, you don't have a chance if a cat decides you're his person!

Another variation on the theme of adopting a new pet is the belief some people have that the previous animal companion either brought the new one or led them to him. Sometimes, the animal will appear in a dream with the pet who is to become the newest member of the family. In our book, *Angel Animals: Divine Messengers of Miracles*, Allen tells about the dream he had of our dear dog Prana carrying our cute little puppy-to-be, Taylor, in her mouth and emerging with her from the ocean. In the dream, Prana deposited Taylor on the beach at Allen's feet. The next day, when we had to figure out which adorable puppy to choose from a litter, Allen recognized Taylor as the dog Prana had selected for us.[15]

TRY THIS EXERCISE

As you think about adopting another pet, imagine how you will introduce the new animal into your home.

- Will you follow some of the same routines?
- Will you buy new food bowls and toys to get a fresh start?
- Can you imagine yourself telling the new animal about his predecessor?

- Will you show pictures of your previous pet to the new one?
- How will you assure your newest member of the family that he can be an individual and doesn't have to try to replace the pet who is no longer with you?

DO ANIMALS REINCARNATE?

Many people wonder about reincarnation. Unless you have experienced it, you probably won't believe reincarnation of souls into a new animal body is possible. But many people have had a childhood pet return as another animal later in life. Sometimes the animal communicates to the person that he will be returning and even tells her what he will look like and when he will be back. The details are so vivid that the person considers the experience indisputable.

A California woman named Sirod wrote to us about her experience with a reincarnated pet.

Years ago, I had a black-and-white cat named Sox. He was very sweet but quiet. I always wished he would speak up a little more for things he wanted. But at only one year old, Sox got sick and died.

A couple of years later, I had a dream about a black-and-white cat coming through a hole in my kitchen wall and dropping onto the table. I heard the words: "He's the one you're waiting for." I wasn't quite sure what those words meant. That is, until years later, when one day, I set out for the animal shelter with the intention of rescuing a cat and bringing him home to be a friend for my other cat, Channel.

I got lost twice while trying to find the animal shelter. I gave up, believing there was a reason for my not getting a cat that day. A week later, on a whim, I stopped at the local pet shop. In the Cats for Adoption cage, there was a black-and-white cat who was about three months old. When the volunteer put the cat in my arms, the kitten just stayed there. He didn't try to get away like a kitten usually would.

I brought the black-and-white cat home. The next morning I awoke to find him inches away and staring into my eyes. When I looked into his eyes, I said, "Oh my God, your eyes are just like Sox's!" With that, the kitten took his paw and gently stroked my cheek. I knew that he had been the one I was waiting for. I named him Spirit. And now, in his new body, he's the noisiest cat in the world. He never shuts up, and I love hearing him speak.[16]

MEDITATION

Come Back to Me

If you wish, ask your animal companion who has died if she wants to return. If she does, ask her to let you know when she is back and how to find you. Visualize yourself looking into the eyes of the new pet and seeing the same spirit gazing back at you.

MEDITATION

The Transition from Life to Living Again

Dear one, if you want to return to me in a new body at another time, always know that you have a place in my heart. All I ask is that you let me know you are here and where I can find you. I will joyfully bring you back home, and we will share a life together again.

How will I know you are here?

What will you look like?

When will it be best for us to reunite?

Afterword

Animal companions love in ways that confound the skeptics, inspire the poets, and outshine the mystics. Their loss can never be restored. Their presence can never be forgotten. But you learn from them to transcend death and to walk through its portal with courage.

We hope this book has helped you to move from sorrow and grief into a place of peace and comfort.

Honor your animal companion. Remember all that you loved and all that you miss. Celebrate a life well lived.

Do what your animal friend would want for you: Love still. Love again. Love forever.

Appendix
Additional Meditations

I REMEMBER YOU

Remembering honors your life and heals my spirit. Remembering creates appreciation and gratitude – two of the most wondrous salves for my secret sorrows.

I know that grief will have its day. I give myself permission to heal the wounds with remembrance of you.

What do I remember most about you?

Why am I remembering this today?

How will my memories of you help me to heal?

THE COURAGE TO REMEMBER

I was honored to be present as you left your physical body. It takes courage to remember what it was like to be with you in your final moments. These painful memories of your death may become my greatest healing agent.

I imagine that at your death, your spirit leaped out of your body. I see you now – released and living happily without pain or suffering.

What do I remember about seeing you die?

What could I see spiritually that did not appear physically?

MEMORIES OF DAILY LIFE

The details of what I remember about you will become stepping-stones across my stream of grief. I remember your unique personality, intelligence, and quirky ways. I vividly recall both the highs and lows of our relationship. I even remember the special foods you loved and how much you enjoyed treats. I still feel you sleeping close to me and all the comfort that your nearness brought to my nights.

I rejoice in and accept that whatever memories float to the surface are worthy of my attention, no matter how trivial they may seem to be. The daily routines and rituals we shared will be exactly what I need to recall for restoring myself.

OUR SONG

There is a song that always makes me think of you. The words to this song express how you made me feel and what you brought into my life.

I like to sing that song out loud or in my mind and think of you. I see your face as I listen to and sing our song. While I relax into the music, I remember how special you were. The song that was our life together will never die.

THE GOLDEN THREAD OF LOVE

My dear departed companion, you have reminded me that we are all connected by a golden thread of love that weaves invisibly through life's fabric.

I will now gently think about your purpose in my life.

How did you make me feel connected to all life?

Why were you with me during this phase of my life?

Has some other cycle ended that coincides with your passing?

FRIENDS AND FAMILY

I need family members and caring friends talking and listening to me about your love and devotion to me and to them. I will get their testimonials in writing and record them in my heart.

What support am I grateful to receive as I mourn the loss of you?

THE REST OF OUR ANIMAL FAMILY

Your animal family misses you. We all need time to grieve. I am watching the reactions of our other pets to your loss. Sometimes I am reminded of my own ways of handling grief.

I will talk to the rest of our animal family and tell them how you died. I will bring images to mind that will reassure them and myself that you are okay now.

What can I say and do to help your animal friends adjust to your absence?

MY NEEDS NOW THAT YOU ARE GONE

You filled many of my physical, emotional, psychological, and spiritual needs. I felt like a complete person with you nearby.

I must fill the holes left by your loss. I need to satisfy in other ways the roles you played as my caretaker, child, and best friend.

How will I fill the needs that you used to take care of for me so I can stop feeling so empty?

YOU MADE ME LAUGH

I remember those times when you caused me to laugh. Because of your playfulness and how you coaxed me into having fun, you added humorous dimensions to my life.

Your ability to turn everyday objects into toys and to get me to play with you reminded me that having fun is essential for a joyful life.

At which times during the day, when I tend to feel especially tense, could I remember what you taught me about play and keeping my sense of humor?

PEACEFUL, AT LAST

The loss of you can never be restored. I can never forget your presence. But I can recover and heal from my profound pain by celebrating a life well lived.

How am I now at peace with your passing? What will I do to give to others the love that you gave to me?

Notes

INTRODUCTION

Epigraph: Theodosia Garrison, "The Closed Door," in *The Best Loved Poems of the American People*, ed. Hazel Felleman (New York: Doubleday, 1936), p. 544.

RAINBOWS

Epigraph: Sir Walter Scott, "Marmion" (canto 6, stanza 5), quoted from http://www.worldofquotes.com/author/Sir-Walter-Scott/1/index.html.

CHAPTER ONE: RAINBOW BLUE

Epigraph: Henry Willett, "In Memoriam," in *The Dog's Book of Verse*, ed. Jo Earl Clausen (Boston: Small Maynard and Co., 1916), quoted in Laurel E. Hunt, ed., *Angel Pawprints: Reflections on Loving and Losing a Canine Companion; An Anthology of Pet Memorials* (New York: Hyperion, 2000), p. 122.

1. Allen M. Schoen, *Kindred Spirits: How the Remarkable Bond Between Humans and Animals Can Change the Way We Live* (New York: Broadway Books, 2001), p. 254.

2. Jamie Quackenbush and Denise Graveline, *When Your Pet Dies: How to Cope with Your Feelings* (New York: Simon & Schuster, 1985), p. 29.

3. Julia A. Harris, *Pet Loss: A Spiritual Guide* (New York: Lantern Books, 2002), p. 31.

4. Wallace Sife, *The Loss of a Pet* (New York: Howell Book House, 1993), p. 115.

5. Sandra, *Angel Animals Story of the Week*, June 22, 2003.

6. Diana Stewart-Koster, *Angel Animals Story of the Week*, June 29, 2003.

7. Rita Teo, ibid.

8. Dee Gurnett, ibid.

9. Trisha Lamb, ibid., July 12, 2003.

10. Sonya Fitzpatrick and Patricia Burkhart Smith, *What the Animals Tell Me: Developing Your Innate Telepathic Skills to Understand and Communicate with Your Pets* (New York: Hyperion, 1997), pp. 192–93.

11. Barbara Charland, *Angel Animals Story of the Week*, January 5, 2003.

12. Marty Tousley, ibid., January 12, 2003.

13. Carol Corville Horn, ibid., January 19, 2003.

14. Barbara Charland, ibid., January 19, 2003.

15. Kim Sheridan, *Animals and the Afterlife: True Stories of Our Best Friends' Journey beyond Death* (Escondido, CA: EnLighthouse Publishing, 2003), pp. 224–25.

16. Rita M. Reynolds, *Blessing the Bridge: What Animals Teach Us about Death, Dying, and Beyond* (Troutdale, OR: NewSage Press, 2001), p. 141.

17. Robert Frost, "Acquainted with the Night," *Complete Poems of Robert Frost* (New York: Holt, Rinehart, and Winston, 1964), p. 324.

18. Joan Rivers, *Bouncing Back: I've Survived Everything. . . and I Mean Everything. . . and You Can Too!* (New York: Harper-Collins, 1997), p. 170.

CHAPTER TWO: RAINBOW RED

Epigraph: Frances Hodgson Burnett, *A Little Princess* (New York: HarperCollins, 1964), p. 15.

1. J. Allen Boone, *Kinship with All Life* (San Francisco: Harper-SanFrancisco, 1954), p. 56.

2. Constance Jenkins, "Request from the Rainbow Bridge (in loving memory of Isolde Jenkins, 1992)," quoted in Hunt, *Angel Pawprints*, p. 156.

3. Sheryl Jordan, *Angel Animals Story of the Week*, January 19, 2003.

4. Christine Davis, *For Every Dog an Angel* (Portland, OR: Lighthearted Press, 2004), p. 10.

5. Pamela Jenkins, *Angel Animals Story of the Week*, August 21, 2004.
6. N. N. Glatzer, ed., *Martin Buber: The Way of Response; Selections from His Writings* (New York: Shocken Books, 1966), p. 99.

CHAPTER THREE: RAINBOW YELLOW

Epigraph: James Whitcomb Riley, "He Is Not Dead," in Felleman, *The Best Loved Poems of the American People*, p. 532.
1. Alan D. Wolfelt, *When Your Pet Dies: A Guide to Mourning, Remembering, and Healing* (Fort Collins, CO: Companion Press, 2004), p. 29.
2. Sife, *The Loss of a Pet*, p. 141.
3. Martin Goldstein, *The Nature of Animal Healing: The Definitive Holistic Medicine Guide to Caring for Your Dog and Cat* (New York: Ballantine, 1999), p. 313.
4. Rupert Sheldrake, *Dogs That Know When Their Owners Are Coming Home: And Other Unexplained Powers of Animals* (New York: Crown Publishers, 1999), p. 97.
5. Shirley MacLaine, *Out on a Leash: Exploring the Nature of Reality and Love* (New York: Atria Books, 2003), p. 138.
6. Burnett, *A Little Princess*, p. 141.

BRIDGES

Epigraph: Albert Schweitzer, *The Animal World of Albert Schweitzer: Jungle Insights into Reverence for Life*, trans. and ed. Charles R. Joy (Boston: Beacon Press, 1951), p. 44.

CHAPTER FOUR: COVERED BRIDGES

Epigraph: Abraham Lincoln, "Memory," in Felleman, *The Best Loved Poems of the American People*, p. 541.

1. Rivers, *Bouncing Back*, p. 87.
2. Harris, *Pet Loss*, p. 89.
3. Wolfelt, *When Your Pet Dies*, p. 27.
4. Marta Williams, *Learning Their Language: Intuitive Communication with Animals and Nature* (Novato, CA: New World Library, 2003), p. 192.
5. Reynolds, *Blessing the Bridge*, pp. 123, 125.
6. Ibid., p. 125.
7. Fred Rogers, *When a Pet Dies* (New York: Putnam and Grosset Group, 1988), p. 1.
8. Linda M. Peterson, *Surviving the Heartbreak of Choosing Death for Your Pet* (West Chester, PA: Greentree Publishing, 1997), p. 67.
9. Sife, *The Loss of a Pet*, p. 100.

CHAPTER FIVE: SWINGING BRIDGES

Epigraph: Helen Keller, *The Story of My Life: With Her Letters (1887–1901)* (New York: Doubleday and Company, Inc., 1905), p. 35.

1. Lincoln Newton Kinnicutt, "Dear Dogs," *To Your Dog and to My Dog* (Boston: Houghton Mifflin, 1915), quoted in Hunt, *Angel Pawprints*, p. 108.
2. MacLaine, *Out on a Leash*, p. 53.

3. Goldstein, *The Nature of Animal Healing*, p. 282.
4. Pat O'Cotter, "A Malamute Dog," in Felleman, *The Best Loved Poems of the American People*, p. 587.
5. Carrie Gilshen, *Angel Animals Story of the Week*, February 23, 2003.
6. The Reverend Mary Piper, "A Moose Messenger," in Allen and Linda Anderson, *God's Messengers: What Animals Teach Us about the Divine* (Novato, CA: New World Library, 2003), pp. 83–84.
7. Rabbi Balfour Brickner, quoted in Sife, *The Loss of a Pet*, p. 139.
8. Eugene O'Neill, "The Last Will and Testament of Silverdene Emblem O'Neill," in Travis Bogard, ed., *The Unknown O'Neill* (New Haven, CT: Yale University Press, 1988), quoted in Hunt, *Angel Pawprints*, p. 73.
9. Harris, *Pet Loss*, p. 9.

CHAPTER SIX: MEMORIAL BRIDGES

Epigraph: Fyodor Dostoevsky, *The Brothers Karamazov*, trans. Richard Pevear and Larissa Volokhonsky (New York: Alfred A. Knopf, 1990), p. 319.
1. Vineeta Anand, *Angel Animals Story of the Week*, March 9, 2003.
2. "I Sing for the Animals," a poem of the Teton Sioux, in June Cotner, *Animal Blessings: Prayers and Poems Celebrating Our Pets* (San Francisco: HarperSanFrancisco, 2000), p. 152.
3. Job 12:7–10, *King James Bible* (New York: American Bible Society, 2001), p. 504.
4. Genesis 9:12–17, *Good News Bible: The Bible in Today's English*

Version (Nashville: Thomas Nelson, Inc., American Bible Society, 1976), p. 9.

5. Grace Strong Dignowity, "To Roxy," ca. 1935, quoted in Hunt, *Angel Pawprints*, p. 80.

6. Ecclesiastes 3:19–21, *The Tanach* (Philadelphia: Jewish Publication Society, 1917), p. 989.

7. Psalm 65:12–13, *Good News Bible*, p. 588.

CHAPTER SEVEN: GOLDEN BRIDGES

Epigraph: Janis Amatuzio, *Forever Ours: Real Stories of Immortality and Living from a Forensic Pathologist* (Novato, CA: New World Library, 2004), p. 195.

1. Williams, *Learning Their Language*, p. 196.

2. Sheridan, *Animals and the Afterlife*, p. xiii.

3. Fitzpatrick and Smith, *What the Animals Tell Me*, p. 24.

4. Williams, *Learning Their Language*, p. 200.

5. Catholic Online, "Saint Martin de Porres," www.catholic.org/saints/saint.php?saint id=306.

6. Harold Klemp, *A Cosmic Sea of Words: The ECKANKAR Lexicon* (Minneapolis: Eckankar, 1998), p. 163.

7. The Venerable Khyongla Rato Rinpoche, quoted in Sife, *The Loss of a Pet*, p. 146.

8. Carrie Gilshen, *Angel Animals Story of the Week*, May 18, 2003.

9. Margaret Neylon, ibid., May 29, 2004.

10. Nory McCluskey, ibid., August 24, 2003.

11. William Nicholson, *Shadowlands* (New York: Fireside Theatre, 1989), p. 130.

12. E. B. White, *Charlotte's Web* (New York: Harper, 1952), p. 164.
13. Christine Davis, *Angel Animals Story of the Week*,
    September 21, 2003.
14. Nancy Miller, ibid., September 7, 2003.
15. Allen and Linda Anderson, *Angel Animals: Divine Messengers
    of Miracles* (Novato, CA: New World Library, 2007),
    pp. 256–59.
16. Sirod, *Angel Animals Story of the Week*, June 9, 2002.

Resources

T his section offers only a small selection of resources for continuing your journey through grieving and healing from the
loss of your animal friend. For additional resources, including rec-
ommended books, audiovisual materials, organizations, services, and
products, or to post memorials and pet obituaries, visit www.saying
goodbyetoyourangelanimals.com.

BOOKS

Moira Anderson Allen, MEd, *Coping with Sorrow on the Loss of Your
Pet*, 20th Anniversary ed. (Indianapolis: Dog Ear Publishing,
2007). This book is another classic on the subject of pet loss

and bereavement, written by a former editor of *Dog Fancy* magazine. In addition to good basic information on grieving and pet loss, the book includes strong sections on how to find missing pets and making a will to provide for your pets. (See p. 140 for information about Moira Anderson's website, the Pet Loss Support Page.)

Mary Buddemeyer-Porter, *Will I See Fido in Heaven? Scripturally Revealing God's Wonderful Non-Human Eternal Plan for His Creatures* (Manchester, MO: Eden Publications, 2000, 2005), P.O. Box 789, Manchester, MO 53022, www.creatures.com and www.petlossbooks.com. Buddemeyer-Porter offers comforting theology from a variety of editions of the Bible especially for Christians who want reassurance that their animals will be in heaven.

Christine Davis, *For Every Dog an Angel*, illus. by Christine Davis (Portland, OR: Lighthearted Press, 2003), P.O. Box 90125, Portland, OR 97290. So many people have found comfort in this little book and its companion, *For Every Cat an Angel*. The illustrations are delightful. The books were inspired by Christine's relationship with the animal she calls her "forever dog," Martha.

Julia A. Harris, *Pet Loss: A Spiritual Guide* (New York: Lantern Books, 2002). This thorough book on the stages of grief has strong sections on how to conduct mourning rituals and ceremonies as well an excellent explanation of various religious teachings on animals and the afterlife.

Laurel E. Hunt, ed., *Angel Pawprints: Reflections on Loving and Losing a Canine Companion; An Anthology of Pet Memorials* (New

York: Hyperion, 2000), and June Cotner, *Animal Blessings: Prayers and Poems Celebrating Our Pets* (San Francisco: Harper-SanFrancisco, 2000). These two books are wonderful resources for poems, essays, and eulogies to comfort you and to use in your pet memorial service.

Gary Kowalski, *Goodbye, Friend: Healing Wisdom for Anyone Who Has Ever Lost a Pet* (Novato, CA: New World Library, 2006). Written by a popular author who is the minister of the Unitarian Universalist church in Burlington, Vermont, this book includes a good section on rituals, ceremonies, spiritual guidance, and readings and poems to use for pet memorial services. It addresses grieving for the entire family — adults, children, and animals — with stories and comforting thoughts.

Mary and Herb Montgomery, *Good-bye My Friend: Grieving the Loss of a Pet*, illus. by Judy King (Minneapolis: Montgomery Press, 1999), and *A Final Act of Caring: Ending the Life of an Animal Friend* (Minneapolis: Montgomery Press, 2003), P.O. Box 24124, Minneapolis, MN 55424. These two booklets are ideal for veterinarians to give to clients. Simple, easy to read, sensitively written, and beautifully illustrated, they give brief introductions to making decisions about euthanasia, burying a pet, and grieving with your human family over the loss of an animal family member.

Jamie Quackenbush, MSW, and Denise Graveline, *When Your Pet Dies: How to Cope with Your Feelings* (New York: Simon & Schuster, 1985). Written by the nation's first full-time pet bereavement counselor, this book has excellent sections to help you evaluate the roles an animal companion played in your life so you can understand how to fill in the gaps left by his absence. It also deals well with bereavement caused by lost pets and the special issues of helping children deal with pet loss.

Rita M. Reynolds, *Blessing the Bridge: What Animals Teach Us about Death, Dying, and Beyond*, foreword by Gary Kowalski (Troutdale, OR: NewSage Press, 2000), www.blessingthebridge.com. This book contains all you could ask for to help you let go of the animals you love, including how to comfort and communicate with the other pets in your family and healing grief with flower remedies, chants, colors, and music. Reynolds runs an animal sanctuary and is establishing a hospice program for animals and humans. This book glows with her kind heart.

Joan Rivers, *Bouncing Back: I've Survived Everything. . . and I Mean Everything. . . and You Can Too!* (New York: HarperCollins, 1997). Rivers, the internationally known celebrity and comedian, offers wonderful, practical, humorous advice about grief and recovery from any kind of loss.

Niki Behrikis Shanahan, *There Is Eternal Life for Animals: A Book Based on Bible Scripture* and *The Rainbow Bridge: Pet Loss Is Heaven's Gain* (Tyngsborough, MA: Pete Publishing, 2002 and 2007, respectively), P.O. Box 282, Tyngsborough, MA 01879, www.eternalanimals.com. These are comforting books for Christians who want biblical proof that they will meet their animal companions in heaven. Well researched and heartfelt, the books were inspired by the author's bereavement over the death of her cat, Pete, and what she identified as a "cross of snow" that appeared in her backyard, reassuring her that animals also have the promise of eternal life. (See p. 141 for information about the author's website, There Is Eternal Life for Animals.)

Kim Sheridan, *Animals and the Afterlife: True Stories of Our Best Friends' Journey beyond Death* (San Diego: Hay House, 2006). Great research! Sheridan organizes hundreds of inspiring stories into stimulating sections about animals who return to let their human friends know that only the physical body has died.

Wallace Sife, PhD, *The Loss of a Pet*, 3rd ed. (New York: Howell Book House, 2005). This is one of the classic books on pet loss, written by a psychotherapist who has specialized in and been recognized as an expert on pet bereavement. The book contains an excellent chapter, "Religion and the Death of Pets," to help you understand various theological positions on the death and afterlife of animals. It also has a good section on the practical aspects of making final arrangements. Dr. Sife is founder and current chairman and treasurer of the Association for Pet Loss and Bereavement. (See p. 139 for contact information for the Association for Pet Loss and Bereavement.)

Alan D. Wolfelt, PhD, *When Your Pet Dies: A Guide to Mourning, Remembering, and Healing* (Fort Collins, CO: Companion Press, 2004), 3735 Broken Bow Road, Fort Collins, CO 80526, www.centerforloss.com. This book is written by an author who is recognized around the world as an expert on grief and mourning. He combines compassion with practicality, giving excellent guidance through the grieving process with a chart that lists characteristics to help you determine if you have dipped from normal grief into clinical depression.

AUDIO RESOURCES

Deborah Antinori, MA, RDT, LPC, *Journey through Pet Loss*, rev.
ed., edited by Joyce Wallace, MEd, CAG, LCSW (Basking
Ridge, NJ: YokoSpirit Publications, 2000), www.petlossaudio
.com. This Audie Award–winning tape was named a *Foreword*
magazine book of the year. It offers an excellent presentation,
with Antinori's soothing voice (she is a professional actor as
well as a therapist) and her wise counsel. She presents essential
information about the stages of grief and how to move through
them. The inclusion of stories about her own losses lets you
know that she relates to what you are feeling without overwhelming you with her sorrow.

CHILDREN'S BOOKS

Debby Morehead, *A Special Place for Charlee: A Child's Companion
through Pet Loss*, illus. by Karen Cannon (Broomfield, CO: Partners in Publishing, 1996), 5023 W. 120th Avenue, Suite 268,
Broomfield, CO 80020. A family holds a memorial service and
creates a scrapbook of memories for a little boy's best dog
friend, Charlee, in this very comforting and informative book.
Marjorie Blain Parker, *Jasper's Day*, illus. by Janet Wilson (Tona-
wanda, NY: Kids Can Press, 2004). This beautifully illustrated
and tenderly written story for K–3 children about the last day
Riley and his family spend with their golden retriever includes
a burial, family memorial service, and memory book con-
structed by Riley.
Fred Rogers, *When a Pet Dies*, photographs by Jim Judkis (New

York: Putnam Juvenile, 1998). What can we say? This book is as wonderful as the late author who wrote it. With great photographs and simple language and concepts, this is a truly helpful book.

FOR PARENTS, CHILD CAREGIVERS, VETERINARIANS, AND TEACHERS

Diane Pomerance, PhD, *When Your Pet Dies*, illus. by Vanessa Mier (Flower Mound, TX: Polaire Publications, 2001), P.O. Box 217, 2221 Old Justin Road, Flower Mound, TX 75028. Easy to read and with touching illustrations, this is a good book for veterinarians to give to grieving children and parents. For each sale, Dr. Pomerance promises to donate one dollar to the SPCA of Texas. For information about her other books, visit www.animal companionsandtheirpeople.com.

Cheri Barton Ross, *Pet Loss and Children: Establishing a Healthy Foundation* (New York: Routledge, 2005). One of the best and most comprehensive books on the subject, this resource contains new information specifically for today's families. It deals well with special types of pet loss, such as through divorce, accidental death or injury, or pets who have gone missing, and with animals who have helped children with illnesses or disabilities. It has good information on what and what not to say and do with children as they struggle to cope with pet loss, and strong sections on the use of art, play, storytelling, and family therapy techniques.

Marty Tousley, *Children and Pet Loss: A Guide for Helping* (Phoenix: Our Pals Publishing Company, 1996). This twenty-page booklet from the Companion Animal Association of Arizona is a practical tool for physicians, veterinarians, teachers, counselors, parents, grandparents, and others who are in a position to help children understand and cope with the loss of a pet. It explains children's attachment to pets and the significance of this type of loss. (See p. 140 for more information about Tousley's website, Grief Healing.)

JOURNALS

David and Kate Marshall, *The Book of My Pet: In Celebration of Pets* (New York: Hyperion, 2000). Questions, prompts, and inspiring quotes take a person through cherished memories of a pet from birth through living together to death and grieving.

Enid Samuel Traisman, MSW, foreword by Herbert Nieburg, *My Personal Pet Remembrance Journal* (Portland, OR: Dove Lewis Emergency Animal Hospital, 1997). This fill-in journal, with wonderfully detailed and thoughtful questions, will guide readers through the journey from death to reconciliation in the grieving process.

ORGANIZATIONS

The Animal Love and Loss Network (ALLN), http://www.alln.org According to its website, the ALLN seeks to bring together those who are mourning the injury, illness, or loss of an animal companion. The network also represents and supports those who are working to end the exploitation and suffering of all animals. This goal is to be accomplished through the open dialogue and free exchange of ideas by a network of caring individuals who

are dedicated to helping themselves and others better understand and move through the pain of grief and loss.

The Association for Pet Loss and Bereavement, Inc. (APLB),
http://www.aplb.org/
Founded by Wallace Sife, PhD, the APLB is a compassionate
nonprofit organization dedicated to helping people during this
very special kind of bereavement. It is constantly improving
and publicizing all of the services available concerning the loss
of a pet. According to its website, the APLB is the only organization in the world doing this.

Best Friends Sanctuary, http://www.bestfriends.org
This organization is not solely dedicated to pet loss and grief,
but you can publish your pet memorial there.

Delta Society: The Human/Animal Health Connection,
http://www.deltasociety.org/
The Pet Loss and Bereavement section, at http://archive.delta
society.org/AnimalsHealthPetLossHotline.htm, has information about pet loss, including sections called "Pet Loss Resource Persons, Counselors, and Groups," which lists people
and organizations by state, and "Pet Loss Support Hotlines
/Telephone Support."

International Association of Pet Cemeteries (IAPC), http://www
.iaopc.com/. Street address: 13 Cemetery Lane, Box 163, Ellen-
burg Depot, NY 12935.
According to its website, the IAPC is a not-for-profit organization dedicated to the advancement of pet cemeteries everywhere
through public-awareness programs. The IAPC was founded in
1971 in Chicago by Pat Blosser. Member pet cemeteries are

expected to maintain the highest business and ethical standards. IAPC operates on a budget that is supported only by dues and other contributions from members. It has no paid employees; all efforts are completely voluntary.

WEBSITES

Grief Healing, http://www.griefhealing.com

Marty Tousley, a hospice bereavement counselor and author, founded this site. Tousley says, "I help individuals and families understand and cope with their grief in the first year following the death of their loved ones. As a volunteer in my community, I also help adults and children. I've designed this website to meet the needs of those who are grieving the loss of their loved ones, whether human or animal. Whatever your particular circumstances may be, I hope that you will feel welcome, and that you will find some comfort here."

In Memory of Pets: Beyond Life's Gateway, http://www.in-memory -of-pets.com/

John E. Mingo, Sr., created this website on November 8, 1997, "in memory of Candy."

Interfaith Association of Animal Chaplains, http://www.animal chaplains.com

Nancy J. Cronk founded this wonderful organization to give official ministry to people going through pet loss. According to its website, the organization's mission is "bringing people of faith together for the love of animals." These chaplains offer pet loss bereavement resources, pet memorial and funeral services, animal blessings, and an online spiritual meeting place for animal lovers.

Pet Loss Grief Support, http://www.petloss.com/
This is a gentle and compassionate website for pet lovers who are grieving over the death of a pet or dealing with an ill pet. Here you will find personal support, thoughtful advice, the Monday Pet Loss Candle Ceremony, tribute pages, healing poetry, and much more.

Pet Loss Support Page, http://www.pet-loss.net
This site was developed by author Moira Anderson Allen, MEd, for anyone who considers a pet a beloved friend, companion, or family member and knows the intense pain that accompanies the loss of that friend.

Rainbows Bridge, http://www.rainbowsbridge.com
Rainbows Bridge is an interactive virtual memorial home for your departed animal companion, in loving tribute to all God's creatures who filled your life with joy, happiness, and love.

Remember Our Pets, http://www.rememberourpets.com
Here you can share the cherished memories of your pet with others and create a cyberspace memorial — a special place you can return to again and again. It's operated by BowTie, Inc., Animal Network.

There Is Eternal Life for Animals, http://www.eternalanimals.com
Niki Behrikis Shanahan designed this site to offer comfort and services to Christians who are mourning the death of their pets.

Acknowledgments

Our deep appreciation to Vanessa Brown, New World Library editor, who was inspired by the loss of her dear cat, Babette, to ask us to write this book so it could help others with their losses. And also to Georgia Hughes, who edited the book with her graceful and sensitive style. We are grateful to copy editor Jacqueline Volin, type designer Tona Pearce Myers, cover designer Tracy Pitts, our fantastic publicist Monique Muhlenkamp, and the wise marketing director and associate publisher Munro Magruder.

Special thanks to Harold and Joan Klemp for inspiring us to share stories about the animal–human spiritual connection.

Love and gratitude to all those who have contributed their comments, stories, and endorsements to this book.

We also extend our heartfelt gratitude to Stephanie Kip Rostan of Levine-Greenberg Literary Agency, Inc., our amazing literary agent.

Barbara Morningstar has been invaluable with her insights about grief and mourning and for introducing us to Dr. Alan D. Wolfelt's wonderful work.

We appreciate the encouragement and support of Barbara Buckner, Arlene and Aubrey Forbes, Josse Ford, Daniel Tardent, Sheila Bontreger, and Barbara Gislason. Our families instilled a love of animals in us from an early age. Special thanks to Allen's mother, Bobbie Anderson, and Linda's mother, Gertrude Jackson, and to our son and daughter, Mun Anderson and Susan Anderson.

Over the years, thousands of people have shared with us their feelings about losing beloved animal companions. Without their honesty and willingness to communicate we would have only had our personal experiences to help us with this book. So thanks to the Angel Animals Network visitors and *Angel Animals Story of the Week* readers for their letters and stories.

And last but not least, thanks to our animal editors: Leaf, Speedy, Cuddles, and Sunshine. Without you, we wouldn't know what animals think.

About
Allen and Linda Anderson

Allen and Linda Anderson are a husband-and-wife writing team and the founders of the Angel Animals Network (www.angelanimals.net). They are the authors of an ongoing book series focused on the miraculous powers of animals for healing, unconditional love, and companionship. They also offer a free email newsletter, *Angel Animals Story of the Week*. The Andersons are clergy members and pet experts who travel around the country speaking to animal organizations, businesses, colleges, and churches. They are contributing authors and hosts of the Angel Pets Fan Club at Beliefnet.com. Their "Pet's Corner" is in *Awareness* magazine, and they write a Reader's Blog for the *Seattle Post-Intelligencer*.

The Andersons are writing instructors at the Loft Literary Center in Minneapolis. In 2004 they were recipients of a Certificate of Commendation from the governor of Minnesota in recognition of their contributions as authors to the State of Minnesota. Their book *Rescued: Saving Animals from Disaster* won the American Society of Journalists and Authors' Outstanding Book Award. The Andersons' work has been featured twice on NBC's *The Today Show*, as well as on ABC's *Nightly News with Peter Jennings* and *Montel*. They have been the subject of numerous national magazine and wire service articles and have been interviewed for London newspapers and BBC Radio.

Allen and Linda share their home in Minneapolis with a family of animals, including two cats, a dog, and a cockatiel.

Contact Allen and Linda Anderson at:
Angel Animals Network
P.O. Box 26354
Minneapolis, MN 55426
Website: www.angelanimals.net
Email: angelanimals@angelanimals.net